STEP-BY-STEP GARDEN GUIDES

Robert Sulzberger

Herb Gardening

AURA BOOKS

**Step-by-Step
Garden Guides
Herb Gardening**

Robert Sulzberger

German-language edition and
photographs
Gärtnern leicht und richtig
Gartenkräuter
© 1994 BLV Verlagsgesellschaft
mbH, München

English-language edition
© 1995 Transedition Ltd,
Oxford OX4 4DJ, England

Translation:
Ruth Yule/Asgard Publishing Services
Editing:
Asgard Publishing Services, Leeds
Typesetting:
Organ Graphic, Abingdon

This edition published by
Aura Books plc

Printed in 1997 in Dubai

ISBN 0 947793 70 4

Photographic credits
All photographs by the author except:
AKG 4, 5, 6; Clive Nichols 31; Photos
Horticultural 21, 54, 55, 57, 89;
Reinhard 2/3, 30/31, 32/33, 84/85;
Reinhard-Tierfoto back cover right;
Seidl 29 bottom, 70, 82; Skogstad 11;
Stein 7, 16, 24/25, 25; Sulzberger/
Kopp 15, 44; Wildlife Matters front
cover

CONTENTS

History and origins

Herbs are a source of health and well-being that's available to everyone, but our knowledge about them has unfortunately tended to become entangled with folklore.

Sometimes it has seemed altogether lost, particularly among the less well-versed members of the population. The resulting lack of information has meant that many people still suffer from the effects of an unbalanced diet.

Knowledge in the Stone Age

The first descriptions of medicinal plants date from as early as 3000 BC, and are attributed to the Chinese emperor Shen Nung. In Europe, herb seeds have been found in late Stone Age settlements, suggesting that herbs were cultivated there very early on.

The recurring question in this context is how Stone Age people, with no way to analyse or identify the constituent parts of the plants, knew about their healing powers.

One possible explanation for this is that they learned about the harmful and the beneficial effects from experience, but it isn't a very satisfactory answer, even if it seems to fit comfortably with modern thinking and modern methods. Instead we

Natural plant-based remedies are called 'galenic' after Galen, a famous Greek physician in the Roman empire.

Knowledge of herbs with healing powers goes far back into the mists of time, and down the centuries has been greatly deepened by learned and religious people.

should remember that at the dawn of history, humanity was closer to the origins of all existence, and in a sense possessed a direct line to the 'cosmic knowledge'.

We can imagine that at least some individuals could 'see' and intuitively recognise the powers of a plant, just as many animals can. We know that animals instinctively develop a preference for the right herbs when they are ill, and surely no one would wish to deny that human beings, too, can make use of their instincts.

The eventual rise of rationalist thought began at the height of Ancient Greek civilisation. In its wake came a series of great thinkers and scientists such as Hippocrates (after whom the doctors' oath is still named), Theophrastus (successor to Aristotle), Dioscorides (who became famous again through his writings 1,500 years later), and Galen (personal physician to Marcus Aurelius).

All of these people had a powerful influence on the development of herbal medicine for many centuries afterwards. Their achievements were further refined and developed during much later periods, primarily by Arab scientists.

Monks, doctors and botanists

In Europe, knowledge about the properties of herbs was chiefly kept alive in the monasteries. During the Middle Ages, thanks to the monasteries many Mediterranean plants found their way into the gardens of ordinary folk. Benedict of Nursia, Wahlafried Strabo from the island of Reichenau, and the cleverly designed monastery plan at St Gallen, represented important milestones in this development.

St Hildegard of Bingen, again much quoted nowadays, combined existing knowledge, astrological data, her own intuition and new observations into her writings, which were held in high regard.

Before that, Charlemagne's famous pronouncements on country estates, the *capitulare de villis*, had ensured that a large number of plants — including a wide variety of herbs — made their appearance in cottage gardens. The effects of this can still be felt today.

Pastor Kneipp's lectures brought about a renaissance in naturopathy.

In the late Middle Ages, German botanists examined the medicinal herbs more closely and ordered them systematically. Otto Brunsfels, Hieronymus Bock, Tabernaemontanus and Leonhard Fuchs did important work, supported by the Italian doctor Matthiolus, who edited and revised the writings of Dioscorides. In the early 16th century the German doctor Theophrastus Bombastus of Hohenheim, generally better known as Paracelsus, made his mark on knowledge of the medicinal herbs.

The first ordered medical treatise in English, John Gerard's famous *Herball,* was published in 1596; it's still in print today. Nicholas Culpeper's *Physicall Directory* followed in 1649, with detailed information on the effects of a number of plants on various diseases and injuries; it, too, is still available.

After the discovery of America some plants from the New World made an appearance here in Europe. Then, at the end of the 18th century, mechanistic theories finally ousted the older thinking that had combined experience with mysticism and intuition.

The significance of herbs

With the dawn of the scientific age holistic observations, including those about plants, sank into the background. Students of herbal medicine began to concentrate on the active agents involved, which could now be determined by analysis. A German apothecary was among the pioneers of this approach- when he isolated the active agent of the opium poppy, and gave morphine its name.

For scientists, it was fascinating to be able to follow in detail how plant remedies work, and to imitate chemical processes in the laboratory. Many superstitions were demolished as their experiments confirmed and explained relationships that had only been suspected by their predecessors. It became possible to apply remedies more precisely. Better yet, new and amazing discoveries were made.

The active agents were the end products of a secondary metabolic process. This process doesn't produce energy and mass for the plant (the primary task); it creates surplus nutrients which are stored in a harmless form in the plant's tissue. These by-products of metabolism often result in properties that set the plant apart from others; they're responsible for such distinctive characteristics as its individual scent.

Active agents and the character of plants

Today, medicinal herbs are often defined simply in terms of their proven constituents and the effects we can explain; but this analytical approach leads to a dead end. The plants are reduced to known chemicals: their character is neglected, and in the process the spiritual dimension is lost.

However precise the description of the inner ingredients, or of the outward appearance before or during flowering, it cannot really capture the character of a plant. Every species of plant represents a force, a spiritual idea, which runs through its whole development and is already laid down in the first shoot, or in the seed itself.

There are some particularly surprising examples which defy analysis but allow us to feel something of the wisdom of creation. For instance, it has been established in the last few years that sunlight illuminates the psyche, while the lower light levels in winter can produce depressive moods in susceptible people. The flowers of St John's wort, with their golden-yellow faces and delicate rays, are reminiscent of the sun; and their active agents do indeed have calming and anti-depressant effects. We can picture the St John's wort standing at the dry edges of a path or a spinney, capturing the energy of sunlight and passing on its powers. Surprisingly, the analogy holds good in the case of an overdose, when St John's wort causes the symptoms of sunburn and sunstroke.

Lavender offers a rather simpler example. In its case, we can see that the effects all agree with each other; the colour of the flowers, the perfume and the pharmacological constituents are all described as cool and calming.

Examples like these open entirely new perspectives. Rudolf Steiner's philosophical approach, in particular, has helped to broaden our perceptions; among other things, it proposes a link between herbal lore and the cosmic influences of the heavenly bodies.

The chemical analysis of plants sharpens our appreciation of detail, but makes a wider perspective more difficult.

Every species of plant deserves our respect as a part of creation. But the power of the medicinal and seasoning herbs has more of a spiritual component than that of many other species which may have more nutrients but fewer distinctive active agents. As a result, these herbs are also more closely bound up with the physical and spiritual well-being of the human race.

A new lease of life for herbal medicine

In the few ancient third-world cultures that remain intact, 'magicians' who are knowledgeable about herbs still determine the nature of medicine. Now, even in our own society, naturopathy is enjoying increasing popularity, despite noisy objections from some representatives

The flowers of St John's wort store up the power of the sun; an overdose produces symptoms similar to those of sunstroke.

of the established state health-care system.

At the time of Pastor Kneipp, one of the fathers of naturopathic healing, herbs already had an important role to play, and these days no conventionally trained doctor should ignore their gentle healing powers. Because nutritionists, too, are increasingly determined to bring their science to the attention of consumers, herbs have begun to assume great significance in public awareness of health issues.

A note of warning

Of course there are also problems with herbs. Any plant will always contain a wide variety of active agents, some of which are less beneficial to us. However, because so many substances are working together, they can act as a buffer against unwanted side-effects from the pure active agent.

Even so, these complex mixtures, which can vary between

specimens growing in different places, are more difficult to handle. Ever since the time of Paracelsus, we have known that preparations with proven healing properties can also cause injury if they are given in too high a dose.

This is why most people's use of herbal remedies must remain fairly limited. For minor aches and pains there's nothing wrong with using home remedies, relying on our own knowledge and a little patience to save a trip to the doctor. But a herb-gardening book like this one can't provide a foolproof course in self-medication; it can only offer pointers towards a deeper involvement with the healing powers of herbs.

Besides, specialist areas like aromatherapy and homoeopathy really deserve detailed treatment as subjects in their own right; and any attempt to do justice to such complex ideas would go far beyond the scope of a book such as this.

The purpose of this book

Our intention here is above all to explain how you can cultivate each species of plant successfully, and then use it in a way that respects and protects its nature.

In the garden, for example, herbs provide aromatic scents to enchant passers-by; but they are also popular partners in companion planting, and can even help to fertilise the soil and provide protection for other plants.

The purple foxglove supplies a powerful heart drug, not at all suitable for home use.

A possible cure for (almost) every ill

Here we can only touch on the enormous variety of medicinal plant species. Arnica, for instance, is one of the most important herbs for healing wounds, but as it enjoys legal protection in the wild, we can't encourage people to collect it for themselves. Anyway, it's better to leave the cultivation of such delicate plants to the professionals.

The foxglove and the lily-of-the-valley both provide important heart drugs — obviously not something you can safely prescribe for yourself.

They're not alone: nature has provided us with an enormously rich supply of plants that have curative properties. Just the names alone — lungwort, goutweed, scurvy grass or eyebright — give some indication of their possible medical significance. They even include many of the well-known garden beauties such as the rose, madonna lily, iris and peony. However, they all have a more restricted significance for home use, so they can't really be discussed in a book of this scope.

There's no rigid distinction between medicinal and culinary plants. Not all herbs are suitable for use in the kitchen: aphrodisiacs, tranquillisers and ingredients for cosmetics don't have to taste nice. On the other hand, all the culinary herbs, without exception, influence metabolism and general well-being. They make some foodstuffs more digestible, provide vitamins and trace elements, contribute to a general increase in resistance to disease and intervene, sometimes directly, in physiological processes.

But let's concentrate here on the most obvious effects. Culinary herbs can release hidden flavours in some dishes, and bring variety into the menu — especially when you bring them fresh from the garden onto the table!

9

Where herbs grow

Herbs are at home in a huge variety of habitats.

Some species enjoy full sun on a limy, stony subsoil which retains heat. Essential oils and mucilaginous secretions usually develop most readily in dry situations. Species such as ramsons (*Allium ursinum*) grow in the woodland shade, where they're accustomed to a humus-rich soil. Plants containing alkaloids are generally happier in damp surroundings. Others again live at the water's edge — or even, like watercress, in the middle of it, on a wet growing medium.

You can usually find some herb that will flourish in almost any location.

As a result, when you're designing a garden you can fit herbs in almost anywhere. Some, such as hyssop and rue, are well suited to the conditions in a herbaceous bed, and have attractive flowers and foliage that make them ideal for this position. Wormwood, by contrast, is more of a solitary. It grows best in warm, well-drained spots, and doesn't thrive in the company of other plants.

The heat-loving southerners such as thyme, sage and winter savory are best accommodated in a rock garden. So is reflexed stonecrop. Similar conditions can be found in a sheltered corner, in front of a south-facing wall, or in front of a hedge on the northern boundary, but well-drained subsoil is essential.

If you're keen to match the individual requirements of each plant as closely as possible, you should create a nature garden. Here the herbs can form part of a plant community similar to that found in the wild. But you'll need to provide them with a range of habitats. As well as the rock garden they'll need a meadow, a pond (and its bank), wayside and woodland edge environments, semi-shade provided by trees, and (last but not least) the 'rubbish dump' — the weedy corner.

For a nature garden in miniature, consider the herb spiral shown on page 17.

Making herbs part of your design

You may want to design a garden to suit a theme of your own choice. If so, there are still

Deciduous woodland in springtime forms the natural habitat of the white-flowered ramsons, with its scent of garlic.

many ways in which you might include herbs within your overall garden design.

The cottage garden style, for instance, is often imitated. Here formal shapes, represented by round or angular paths and beds, predominate: everything is symmetrical.

The choice of plants, on the other hand, relies on skilful selection to produce a cheerful mixture of colours. Herbs more used to their own company may be planted with cucumbers and tomatoes as companions, or alongside brilliant flowers and fat cabbage heads. Southern-wood, uncommon elsewhere, is

for once allowed to form a low hedge in this garden, while thyme or savory provide an aromatic edge to the borders.

There is also a trend towards using natural materials for paths and fences in cottage gardens, and this suits herbs very well indeed.

Another way to make herbs a part of your garden design has to do with the revival of interest in fragrances. If you want to adopt this as a theme, see to it that people have a chance to

In the cottage garden, herbs mix well with vegetables and flowers.

enjoy scents as frequently as possible. Place plants near the edges of paths, where a delightful waft of perfume can more easily reach the passer-by — but don't plant them too close, or they'll be trodden on. Another good location is next to seats and resting-places, which are also good positions for container-grown plants.

11

Various herbs standing in ordered rows in their own bed — from the left, white peppermint, lemon balm and hyssop.

The herb bed

If you prefer to have all your herbs next to one another, simply put them together in a single garden bed.

Since the cook usually needs these intensely flavoured ingredients frequently, quickly and in small amounts, it's definitely a good idea to site the herb bed near the kitchen. For preference it should be rather narrower than the usual 4 ft (1.2 m), so

that every little herb is always in comfortable reach.

Stepping stones within the bed have the same effect, but put a layer of sand underneath them to keep them stable and prevent accidents. Undressed stone slabs have a particularly attractive natural look.

Growing conditions

When you're thinking about the general growing conditions that herbs are going to need, you should remember that many culinary herbs (and many other garden plants, too) were originally brought from southern countries. Plants native to the Mediterranean or the Orient tend to be used to infertile, free-draining soils and lots of sunshine, and these conditions will

produce the best flavour. Rich soils tend to produce quantity, in the form of green vegetation, rather than quality, in the form of active agents, and in any case, nothing much happens without sunshine. Even so, aim to respect the individual requirements of each herb as far as possible. You'll find these listed in the plant profiles starting on page 34.

If your ground is heavy, you'll need to do something with it to achieve a free-draining subsoil. With soil that's loamy and silty it's often enough to mix in coarse sand, and perhaps a little well-rotted garden compost. With very heavy, clayey soil, it's also worth putting in a drainage layer of gravel at a depth of 8–12 in (20–30 cm), or even making a raised bed and filling it with an artificial growing medium. Plants can take root in this without any risk of water-logging.

To meet the needs of the hungrier plants, you mustn't neglect the topsoil. The essential ingredient is ripe garden compost that's been rotting for at least a year. Its pH value should be between 6.0 and 7.0. In more acid soils apply as much lime as required: this will also help the many lime-loving herbs. And if you have time to sow a soil-enriching crop first, the ground will be prepared as well as it possibly can be.

Planting
The best time for planting is usually in spring (April) or in

autumn (September/October); in either case, cloudy conditions are best. Species vulnerable to frost (e.g. thyme) are better planted in spring.

Young plants are always small, whether you've raised them at home or bought them from the garden centre, but don't be fooled by their size. Herbs can only develop properly if you plant them far enough apart to allow for their final size. This will also save you having to move them later on. However, until the plants reach their full size and cover the soil you'll need to remove weeds before they can inhibit the herbs' development.

Planning and arranging your plants

Try to arrange your plants in such a way that the lower-growing species are at the front and the tallest are at the back. Sunlight, of course, is crucial for growth, so it's best to think of the southern side of your garden as the 'front'. However, you may have to give priority to the direction from which the herbs will be seen, arranging them so that they will increase in height the farther they are from the main path.

If you have plenty of room, you can use more space to create artistic effects.

For example, in these circumstances it's a good idea to plant several examples of any species that has particularly attractive flowers or foliage, and you can even do this if it means you

won't actually need to harvest them all.

Lavender and sage, feverfew, borage, marigold and camomile, are all among the prettier residents of the herb bed, and are often planted in larger numbers. If you don't intend to harvest them, treat them as ornamentals; remove unattractive parts of the plant and cut them back in autumn or spring.

The reflexed stonecrop, being a member of the Crassulaceae family, is a succulent plant that prefers a well-drained position in the rock garden.

Herbs as companion plants

Companion planting is a well-established and successful technique in the organic garden. Now that we know different plant species get on well as neighbours, it's possible to accommodate a larger selection of plants even when space is limited. This does no harm at all: in fact, because the plants effectively complement one another, they can actually promote one another's growth.

For one thing, the available space can be put to optimum use. Big, strong plants can protect their more delicate neighbours from wind and weather. Plants with a spreading habit will cover the ground, ensuring that more water is retained and making it more difficult for weeds to grow there. Under the ground, shallow-rooting and deep-rooting plants complement each other ideally, because each will absorb different nutrients from different levels.

Some species can even protect their neighbours from diseases or pests. To spread from one part of the garden to another, specific diseases must infect the plants of a particular species or botanical family. When herbs belonging to different families are grown as companion plants, they create an effective barrier to infection. So it's worth ensuring that members of the same botanical family don't come up against each other too often.

This applies, for instance, in the case of the Umbelliferae, which are well represented among the vegetables (carrot, celery, celeriac, fennel etc.) and among the herbs (parsley, dill, chervil, caraway, lovage etc.). The same applies to other large families such as the Compositae (most lettuces) and the Cruciferae (cabbages and cress, horse-radish etc.).

Pests can also be sidetracked by strong, unknown odours that mask the smell of their victims. Herbs can often produce this effect, because they contain particularly strong and active chemicals. The following summary gives some examples.

How herbs can protect vegetables

Onions or chives next to carrots — each keeps vegetable flies off the other.

Garlic or onions next to strawberries — protect the strawberries from fungal disease.

Thyme as edging for a bed — keeps snails away.

Wormwood next to currants — guards against rust.

Nasturtium planted under fruit trees — keeps woolly aphids and aphids at bay.

Lavender next to roses — keeps aphids away.

Chives and French marigold — keeps off root-knot nematodes.

14

...eans and savory belong together in ...e vegetable plot as well as in the ...ooking pot.

These are only some of the ...ost obvious protective effects. ...imilar effects can be seen in ...any other instances as well. Parsley and tomatoes, for ...istance, are known to be good ...eighbours, and parsley thrives ...ext to lettuce. Dill is often ...cattered between cucumber ...lants, and when sown in the ...ows with radishes it leads to ...nproved germination.

The commonest such combi-...ation is beans and savory. As ...vell as providing excellent com-...lementary seasoning on the ...linner plate, this interesting ...erb makes an ideal neighbour ...n the vegetable patch.

Plants such as borage and marigold are always welcome visitors in the vegetable plot. Besides their cheerful blue or orange flowers, which are attractive to insects as well as people, the saponins in their roots improve the characteris-tics of the soil. What is more, if

Nasturtiums around their trunks help to keep these trees free of aphids.

you leave either of these species alone, it will both readily and rapidly self-seed.

Herbs can also promote the growth of other herbs, often on a reciprocal basis. For example, herb growers have found that when sage and tarragon are grown next to each other, they develop more intensive sub-stances than if they are left simply to stand alone or among their own kind.

A herb spiral can offer a whole range of habitats — from the well-drained summit, via ordinary garden soil, and on to the moist area on the sunny southern side.

The herb spiral

The herb spiral is much more than a pretty feature. It's the result of a considered attempt to create a variety of conditions in a small space.

The herb spiral provides a whole series of habitats, from a pond at the lowest level to a warm, dry area at the top, to suit the widest possible range of herbs. The result should be an area capable of supporting the highest possible concentrations of essential ingredients within a small space — and you should not have to work too hard to look after them.

When choosing a site, the first essential is to find a sunny spot.. That way a large amount of heat will be stored at the peak of the artificial hill, and in the stones around it. The pond at the bottom should also reflect the sun's rays (provided you dig it on the south side of the spiral), while behind the hill (and the taller-growing species) there'll be cool, shady areas.

You can provide a similarly wide range of growing mediums. From well-drained, chalky, sandy soil at the top, through the fairly normal, humus-rich garden soil of the central zone, to wet soils and pond water, you'll have everything your plants could possibly want.

Large-scale building operations

This won't be an easy task, so before you start, mark out the planned shape of your spiral with pegs. Use string to indicate its final form, and check it one last time before you commit yourself.

Start by removing the grass from the entire area, taking off the topmost soil layer at the same time. It would be a great pity to bury the topsoil, because you're going to need a lot of it later on.

The same logic should apply when you're digging out the pond on the south side. Be sure to separate out the humus-rich topsoil from the subsoil. Most subsoils are low in nutrients but generously supplied with stones.

If the pond takes up 25-30 per cent of the total area, it should look right as a part of your miniature landscape. It also needs to be at least 32 in (80 cm) deep if plants and animals are going to spend the winter in it without getting frozen.

Make sure you organise the building stones you will need for the wall in good time, and preferably well in advance. Natural stones are most suitable

for the purpose, but they're also very heavy. That means your choice inevitably depends on the stones that are available locally.

Always lay your stones in a stable position (flat side down) and bonded, and build the wall so it slopes slightly inwards, into the hillside.

It's a good idea to lay the stones on top of each other, in two or three layers, and then imediately fill the central area with a suitable substrate. That way your handiwork will have the stability it needs right from the start.

The lower layers of substrate should provide easy drainage: use rubble, fragments of stone,

Building a herb spiral is hard work, but the result is a very attractive garden feature.

and humus-free subsoil. On top of this you should lay a sandy growing medium — you can mix it with limestone chippings.

Fill the flatter areas straight away with humus-rich topsoil. If you like, you can improve it by adding some well-rotted garden compost.

In the moist area just above the pond, you should be aiming for a more acid environment. Use leaf mould here, or peat if necessary.

The herb spiral from top to bottom:

Summit area (A): lavender, rosemary, thyme, sage, winter savory, hyssop, reflexed stonecrop

Transitional area (B): basil, sweet marjoram, wild marjoram, yarrow, St John's wort

Middle area (C): bergamot, chives, salad burnet, sorrel, savory, lemon balm, tarragon, dill, caraway, coriander, fennel, lovage, rue, southernwood, camomile, marigold, borage, nasturtium; in semi-shade: parsley, chervil, cress

Moist area (D): various mints (peppermint, pennyroyal etc.), lady's mantle

Water area (pond): watercress, sweet flag, bogbean, water mint

Herbaceous perennials (preferably planted outside the spiral): valerian, mugwort, comfrey, horseradish, wormwood

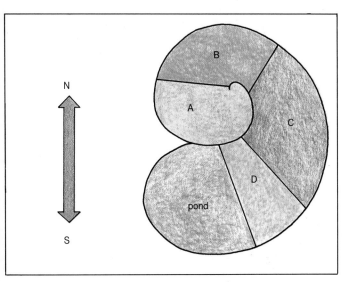

Container-grown herbs

Anyone who wants to, or has no other option, can grow herbs in containers. It isn't difficult to do. The main requirement — plenty of sunshine — is easily met on a balcony or patio (which will often face south). Besides, herbs in containers are easy to move about, and most herbs are happy in nothing more than a thin layer of soil or compost.

There are a few herbs that won't thrive in these conditions — those that grow especially tall, for instance, or that are grown specifically for their roots. Horseradish, valerian and angelica combine both these characteristics, while southern-wood and wormwood are also ill at ease in containers.

However, large individual tubs can help here, and it's fun trying anyway. Rosemary after all is best grown in a tub because it's vulnerable to hard frosts.

When choosing containers, think about the space the plants need for their roots, and think carefully about materials too.

The usual plastic troughs aren't particularly attractive, but they are adequate for most of the smaller species. Terracotta containers bring a touch of the Mediterranean to the terrace. 'Strawberry barrels' — tall terracotta pots with several holes in the side — make ideal herb planters. There's also a smaller version of this, made for

one particular herb and called a 'parsley pot'.

Stone troughs are even heavier than terracotta. Usually there's only room for a little growing medium in these, which makes them ideal for rock-garden plants. Thyme, winter savory, chives and reflexed stonecrop are all well suited to a long-term home in a stone trough, and smaller species such as parsley,

salad burnet, basil and marjoram can widen the selection.

If you build your own container out of wood, you can make the size fit your requirements, and you're rewarded with a planter that looks natural. Paint the whole container with a rotproof paint that is non-toxic to plants, adding a further coat of weatherproof paint on the outside, and the container will last many years. But beware: for herbs, drainage holes for surplus water are even more important than usual!

Filling and planting containers

Most species are vulnerable to waterlogging, so as a general rule you should aim to start with a drainage layer of broken crocks or expanded clay granules right at the bottom of the container.

You can use ordinary potting compost as the growing medium. You can make your own from one part each of sand, well-rotted garden compost and ordinary garden soil. Or alternatively, some kind of bark-based

Above *In a skilfully planted container, there's room for three rows of herbs.*

Left *This sort of container will look very attractive if you plant flowers among the herbs and choose ornamental forms like the yellow-variegated sage.*

or coir compost can also be bought as a substitute.

If you're planting strong feeders such as balm, tarragon, marjoram or borage it's a good idea to mix in a slow-release fertiliser. Supplementary liquid feeds can be given later, as required.

If you take care about planning it, a tub of herbs can be a source of good health that's also very attractive to look at. For example, if the container's wide enough, tall species such as fennel, borage or balm can be placed at the back; dill's rather prone to wind damage, so you should give it some support. Low and trailing herbs such as thyme, land cress, chervil or nasturtium are suitable for the foreground, facing the sun. Plants of medium height, like hyssop or savory, fit nicely in between.

As the compost in containers dries out easily, don't forget to water them well in hot weather. Species that tend to grow tall should be cut back repeatedly; afterwards most will tolerate a supplementary feed. After three years, renew the compost and plant the herb box afresh.

Cultivation methods

The first stages in growing herbs

Herbs are propagated in much the same way as other garden plants.

In some cases, notably the perennial herbs, it's easiest to use vegetative propagation methods such as planting cuttings or pieces of the root.

Annual herbs, on the other hand, can usually be raised from seed, though the more demanding (and the less hardy) species prefer to be started under cover. This not only improves germination, but also gives them more time to develop.

Simply sow direct

If you're planning to sow directly into open ground, wait until the soil has warmed up a little and become friable. This has usually happened by early April. Before sowing, you should break the soil up by hand, clearing it of unwanted wild plants at the same time. At this time of year the ground is moist anyway.

As a rule, the seed should be covered by three times its own depth of soil: bean-like seeds

Freshly sown herb seeds may need watering after a week or so.

Seeds for herbs

Breeding seed strains for culinary herbs — and more particularly for medicinal herbs — hasn't reached anything like the level of sophistication achieved for the innumerable vegetable and flower seeds.

You can buy seed varieties for the more common species, but most herbs have received little attention from plant breeders, and it's often difficult to obtain seed commercially.

In some cases, gardeners have to do the propagation themselves or — within the limits of the law — go and collect the seed from plants in the wild.

Of course, this state of affairs does have some advantages. In the first place, it means that, unlike with many vegetable and cereal species, there's still plenty of natural, unexploited genetic material available. Secondly, it means that herbs develop their ingredients through an interplay with their natural surroundings, which is particularly important for medicinal herbs.

Plant breeders aim for 'standard content', but this is mainly significant in higher dosages, and in industrial applications. It's less important for everyday medicinal use in the home.

can be placed in drills 1¼-1¾ in (3-4 cm) deep, but fine seeds need nothing more than a thin layer of soil sieved over them.

Some seeds are photopositive — i.e. they need light in order to germinate (see directions for

Right *Pricking out basil into a tray: always give your seedlings plenty of room.*

Below *Many species can easily be propagated by layering, or by taking stem cuttings.*

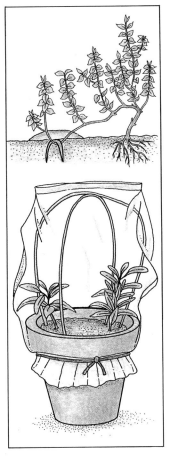

individual species). In such cases it's particularly important not to cover the seeds completely, or they will simply never sprout.

When you draw seed drills in a seed or nursery bed, they can be close together. However, some herbs (e.g. parsley, dill and chervil) are normally left to grow where they are sown. In this case plant the seeds in rows far enough apart to leave room for the mature plants. That way you'll only have to thin plants within the rows.

Don't scatter the seeds too thickly in the first place; finish off by firming and watering them in. Finally, adding a written label will maks it easier to identify the seedlings once they've come up.

The newly sown seeds must never be allowed to dry out, especially during the first few weeks — so in warm, dry weather you should keep watering them regularly. Cover up the soil until the seeds germinate: this helps to keep it moist for longer. If the seeds have been sown close together, then they'll soon need to be thinned, and if you're unlucky may even need to be thinned out a second time round.

If you allow a herb (parsley, in this case) to come into flower, then you can collect seed yourself.

Seeds on a window-sill

Plants from southern lands in particular need to be raised from seed on a warm window-sill or in a greenhouse. You can start this as early as March.. But while they're germinating, they will need all the warmth and protection you can give them — a prime example of this is basil.

Sowing is usually done in shallow pans filled with a light, sandy growing medium that's low in nutrients, such as John Innes seed compost or some proprietary seed compost.

It's a good idea to have suitable holes in the base of the pan, and perhaps a drainage layer too (of broken crocks, clay pellets, or sand). This will ensure that excess water can escape unhindered.

If you sow single seeds straight into the individual cells of a modular system — or into peat jiffy pots — you can save yourself the job of pricking out. at a later stage. A good root ball is formed very quickly, making it easier to transplant the seedlings and grow them on later.

Press the seeds gently into the growing medium, and cover them with a thin layer of seed compost. Water your containers in advance by placing them in a

Plant purchase permitted: it's easier to control quantities when plants are raised in individual pots, and you normally don't need more than a few examples of each herb. For this reason, it's entirely legitimate to buy plants ready raised from the garden centre, rather than sowing at home and having to throw the surplus seedlings away.

shallow tray of water until the moisture has soaked through

and risen to the surface of the compost. If you've done this, you probably won't have to water again until the seeds have germinated. To make sure they retain the moisture they need until then, it's a good idea to cover them with a sheet of glass or clear plastic film, or with a purpose-designed lid.

As soon as the seed leaves are large enough to handle, take the seedlings out and replant them in a light-textured potting compost (if they're not already planted in single pots or cells). The sooner this is done the better. Don't leave it any later than this to put them in individual plant cells; this will help them to form good root balls.

When the young plants are strong enough, they can go outside. It shouldn't get too cold for them after the beginning of May, but you need to harden them off first. Begin by putting them outdoors on overcast days, then on sunny days as well; and finally leave them out at night, but covered with a fleece.

Planting out, too, is better done when it's not too sunny. If the herb is vulnerable to frost it's better to wait until after the end of May, when all danger of frost is past. If seeds have been sown in the summer, it's best to plant out in October.

New plants from old roots

Some herb species tend to lose some of their most desirable characteristics when propagated from seed. For these, the best

Frost-tender species should only be planted out once all danger of frost is past.

(and often the simplest) method is vegetative propagation: using the parts of plants you've already got to produce new ones.

Perennial herbs such as lemon balm, lovage and lavender have the most pressing need: they should be divided about every three to four years. It's done by digging up the roots in spring or in autumn and dividing them with a knife. For tougher rootstocks, use a spade. In simpler cases such as chives, just tear the roots apart with your hands and replant the divided sections in a fresh trench. You could dress the trench with rotted garden compost first.

With some species, root division is particularly easy. Peppermint and marjoram, for example, produce runners along

the soil surface which you can remove for propagation; shoots from the runners should be cut back hard in the process. Where herbs are grown for their roots (e.g. horseradish, angelica, comfrey), you simply take pieces of the fleshy roots. These send up shoots again by themselves.

Putting roots on shoots

Like root division, this way of propagating plants from cuttings is no longer one of gardening's mysteries. It's done in early summer, and works particularly well with shrubby species such as sage, thyme, winter savory, rosemary, lavender, hyssop and southernwood.

Take a sharp knife and cut the tips from non-woody shoots. The cuttings should be 2½–4 in (6–10 cm) long, and cut cleanly just below a leaf or pair of leaves. Remove the leaves from the lower two-thirds of the cutting, and put it in a container with a 50:50 mixture of moist peat (or coir) and sand.

If the whole thing's kept shaded from full sun, roots will form within a few weeks. You can speed up the process by keeping the cutting in a warm, moist atmosphere under a transparent plastic hood (e.g. an inflated plastic bag).

An even simpler method is to take shoots growing near the ground and pin them down below the soil; leave them attached to the parent plant, and their 'umbilical cord' when the roots are well formed. This process is known as layering.

23

Caring for plants the natural way

Natural methods of cultivation are probably more suitable for herbs than for anything else in the garden. If you've planted them in the right place, they don't often need supplementary fertiliser, and their powerful aroma gives them better protection from pests than other species. And if you look after your herbs in the natural way, you'll help make their seasoning and medicinal properties as effective as possible.

Prolonging the garden year

The use of cold frames, plastic film and even greenhouses is a legitimate deviation from the path of nature: all of them bring forward or prolong the herb harvest. They allow you to gather frost-tender species like marjoram as early as the beginning of summer, while the warm situation gives chives, parsley and the winter salad plants an advantage as soon as the main growing season is over. But you shouldn't forget to ventilate and water the plants regularly in sunny weather, or they'll fall victim to heat stress.

Hamburg parsley (grown primarily for its roots) and dandelion can, like chicory, be forced into growth in winter if they're put into tubs in a warm spot. Chive clumps, too, will produce an early crop of their tasty tubular leaves on the window-sill. You can sow chervil, cress and other species grouped together as sprouting seeds in flat containers on the window-sill; they'll even sprout in glass jars, without any growing medium, provided you keep them moist enough. Even in their earliest stage these species serve as a spicy winter green vegetable, rich in vitamins.

Most of the more common perennial herbs are frost-hardy in our latitudes. Some winter salad plants can be harvested right up to the point when snow and frost make it impossible.

However, southerners like thyme or sage are grateful for a protective covering of brushwood or something similar, particularly in exposed positions. Rosemary and bay will usually survive outdoors in open ground, as long as they're growing in a sunny spot sheltered from cold winds. But a severe winter will kill them, so if you have any doubts, keep them in containers that can be brought under cover.

Herbs that appreciate feeding

It's true that some herb species flourish on the most infertile ground in the wild, but this is no reason to neglect their

Chives can be harvested on the window-sill: just allow the root balls to freeze through once, then pot them up.

feeding completely. These species, too, will do better with a well-judged dose of fertiliser. But you need to make some careful distinctions. Herbs, just like other plants, include some hungry species as well.

It *is* true that mass production has no place in the herb bed. There may be plenty of foliage, but that doesn't necessarily mean it'll contain equally generous amounts of the substances you're growing it for. The production of essential oils depends more on the sun than on the availability of nutrients. Apart from that, herbs are very sensitive to what they're feeding on; they show a clear preference for nutrient supplements of organic origin.

There are slow-working, long-lasting fertilisers available for

the purpose, based on hoof-and-horn and dried blood. The various organic complete fertilisers often include phosphorus-rich bonemeal and guano supplements. Home-made liquid fertilisers can provide a quick-acting application of nitrogen (see how to prepare them on pages 94-95).

Well-rotted garden compost is indispensable for providing humus. As a rule, it should have rotted for at least a year so that it doesn't encourage excessively 'stalky' growth. Ideally, you should always apply it at the beginning of the growing season; if plants have been freshly planted, wait a while until strong roots have formed.

Strong herbaceous perennials such as lovage, horseradish, lemon balm and angelica are among the hungrier species of herb — but so are chives, dandelion and sorrel. Indeed, all of these plants will benefit from being given extra nutrients occasionally during the course of the year — that is, in addition to the basic application of fertiliser.

Sprouting vegetables make it possible to extend the gardening year for as long as you like; they also ensure a supply of vitamins for the cold weather.

If you want to pay individual attention to your herbs, there's a useful rule of thumb when it comes to applying fertiliser.

Species grown for their leaves and shoots (particularly plants containing alkaloids) can be given fertiliser that's fairly rich in nitrogen.

Herbs grown for their roots should be fed with the emphasis on potassium.

Plants whose fruit and seeds are harvested will need a fertiliser based on phosphorus.

Don't however, allow this rule to lead you into a totally one-sided application of fertiliser. Besides, since most garden soil is over-supplied with potassium and particularly with phosphorus, fertiliser is mainly needed to supply nitrogen.

the right growing conditions (the correct soil type, the right amount of sun etc.) for the individual species concerned, and as long as you space your plants at the recommended distances.

Moreover, if unpleasant fungi or voracious insects *do* find a way in, you can prepare remedies from other herbs to help you combat them (for details of these, see page 94).

In the herb bed, just as elsewhere in the garden, you should always try to avoid competition from wild plants,

Left *The sharp odours given off by lovage keep pests and diseases away as well.*

Below *In the case of the wormwood, even the currant bush next door will benefit.*

The gardener's dream: plants that will protect themselves

Herbs containing strong aromatics and poisons can prove more than a match for pests and diseases, which tend to leave those herbs in peace. These odours can be so powerful they protect neighbouring plants as well. Thus many herbs have become proven partners in mixed cultivation, among

themselves as well as in the vegetable plot or flower bed (see pages 14-15).

However, some of them, notably lovage and wormwood, contain ingredients with a penetrating, unpleasant smell, and are best planted a little out of the way. Wormwood, at least, has good friends among the currants (see also page 14).

It isn't difficult to protect plants in the herb bed, just so long as you provide them with

Common causes of damage in the herb bed

Snails some herbs are at risk from snails, especially basil (which is why it's best to grow it in a balcony tub or window-box). You can give some protection to other foliage herbs by planting a strongly scented border of thyme, for example, but you can never protect them completely.

Aphids appear particularly often on borage and nasturtium. If they aren't making the entire plant unusable, you can leave them be. In near-natural surroundings, beneficial insects (ladybirds, lacewings, gall-midges etc.) soon appear, and get rid of them longer and more effectively than the 'chemical weapons'. Otherwise, preparations based on soft soap can help.

Mildew occurs as a whitish deposit; it's very frequent on marigolds after prolonged dry weather, or when they're planted too close together. Once mildew attacks, it's too late to do anything about it; as a precaution, always space plants far enough apart.

Rust is also a danger, and for garden mint especially. This fungal infection produces raised rust-coloured spots on the undersides of the leaves. Here too, it's worth ensuring that the plants have plenty of air around them as a preventative measure. If they are attacked, cut them back hard, collecting and destroying fallen leaves and stems.

One possible result of dry weather — an attack of mildew.

which most gardeners would naturally classify as 'weeds'.

However, any chemical preparations are completely inappropriate for a natural, organically grown garden. If you do need to get rid of any of these plants, then you can occasionally use a hoe, which will also have the benefit of loosening the soil.

It's also worth remembering that many of the wild plants — dandelion, for example — also possess healing powers. So you should consider whether at least some of these wild 'visitors' might be made welcome as an indispensible part of the garden-herb community.

27

A successful harvest

Choosing the right moment

Everyone who grows useful plants has a single goal in mind: the harvest. But you shouldn't simply go into the garden and cut down the plants, particularly if those plants are herbs.

If you're going to get as much as possible out of them, and preserve their savour and their valuable ingredients, there are a few things you should know.

At the very least, you need to be familiar with the parts of the plant that will be used for each of the particular purposes you have in mind. Do you gather the

The active agents are usually most plentiful just before the herb comes into flower.

leaves, the flowers, the ripe seed or the whole of the plant above ground? Or will you have to dig up the roots as well?

In most cases we're dealing with foliage herbs (you can find the details in the individual plant profiles). But the rules for harvest given below also apply to herbs where you want the flowers or the seeds.

You can pick leaves from foliage herbs for immediate, everyday use at almost any time during the growing season, only provided the plants are strong enough to tolerate the slight drain on their resources. in this case you don't have to bother about any firm rules; just take what you need.

It's different with the main harvest. Your main aim here, after all, is to get the largest possible stock of the herb in question, and as far as possible to do so when it has the largest available quantity of its valuable constituents.

How much of theses substances the herb actually contains will depend to a large extent on where it's growing and what the weather has been like. Clearly, none of us can have much influence on the weather, but on the other hand we can make use of a few insights related to it.

It is generally known, for instance, that the plants' valuable constituents reach their highest levels *before or at the start of flowering*, and at midday on a typical day. At least, this is true of essential oils. What is more, after just a few sunny days there are substantially more valuable constituents than after a rainy spell.

It isn't only the substances contained in the herbs that are important for the next stage in the process. We also have to consider the physical condition of the plants.

They shouldn't be damp (following rain or morning dew), nor should they be limp from the hot midday sun. So the best time to harvest is late in the morning, on the second of a series of sunny days, as soon as the dew has dried.

Valerian contains a host of medicinally active ingredients, which withdraw back into the roots before the winter begins.

For most herbs, the main harvest should take place in July. Some species can even be cut back several times, because they keep on sending up plenty of shoots.

The best containers to use for collecting the herbs are trugs or baskets in which they can lie loosely; plastic bags simply aren't suitable.

Special cases: seeds and roots

Many of the herbs grown for their seeds are umbellifers such as caraway and coriander. The members of this plant family have a particularly inconvenient characteristic, namely that their seeds don't all ripen at once. So you need to find some way of making sure that half the seeds don't drop out before the last ones are ripe.

There are two ways of achieving this. The first method is to harvest the entire seed-head as soon as the first individual seeds ripen, then hang it up head-down for the rest to ripen (don't forget to put something underneath them).

Alternatively, you can wrap the individual seed-heads in fabric. Provided you do this in good time, you'll be able to catch any of the seeds that drop out early. Finally, once the seeds have all ripened, you can knock the remaining seeds out onto a large underlay, and blow on them gently to separate them from the chaff.

Herb roots should be dug up during the winter half of the year, because this is the season when their active agents have withdrawn into their underground tissues. But you should do this job before the frosts really take hold, which in practice usually means October or November.

The best time of day for the harvesting the roots is early in the morning, because yet more of these valuable substances draw back into the underground parts overnight.

29

Processing and preservation

After harvesting, you'll normally start by washing your crop of herbs. In ideal circumstances, if they're going to be preserved, you should avoid getting leaves and flowers wet again. But these days we seem to be surrounded by exhaust emissions from cars and industry, which do rather spoil one's appetite for anything that hasn't been washed. Take the opportunity at this stage to remove any diseased plant tissue: it's no good for seasoning, and certainly has no medicinal use.

You can't avoid washing roots, and this doesn't cause any problems, either.

Wash leaves under a gentle trickle of lukewarm water, and then, before you do anything else to them, shake them out well and leave them to dry naturally.

Nothing beats freshness!
The best argument for growing your own herbs is the chance it gives you to harvest them fresh from the garden for immediate use. You can chop them finely and sprinkle them on salads, add them to sauces or make a tea. That's the only way you'll be able to enjoy the full natural flavour, and the only way that the seasoning and healing ingredients will keep their full

Drying is the commonest way of making your herb harvest last, but it's best done in the shade!

powers. In practice, some species can only be used in this way; salad herbs (in particular chives and borage) should only be eaten fresh.

If you want herbs available in the cold season, too, and don't want to miss the main harvest,

To cook or not to cook? Some herbs don't release their savour to other foods until they're cooked in with them — whereas others lose valuable constituents if treated this way, so should only be added just before serving. Follow the guidelines given for the individual species.

Put the aromatic essences you have obtained into airtight containers, and label them clearly to avoid unwelcome mix-ups later. Anything that doesn't end up in the freezer should be stored in a cool, dark place.

Drying

Drying has proved a very effective way to keep many of the seasoning and tea herbs for a year or so. Unfortunately it doesn't work for *all* herbs — parsley and dill, for example, lose a lot of their flavour.

However, most herbs that you gather on the stem can be tied up in bunches and hung head down in an airy, shaded place such as a garden shed (with a fan heater), a shaded balcony or an airing cupboard (but not if it's in the kitchen). A plate-warming compartment, or the cool oven of an Aga, are also suitable. In the short term you'll be rewarded with a picturesque addition to the house, and a very pleasant aroma.

Another possible method for leaves, flowers and seeds is to stretch nets or loosely woven fabric on wooden frames and spread your crop over them. You can then put the whole lot into a cool oven or an airing cupboard to dry.

Sage growing in the herb garden of a top-class restaurant – freshly picked is always best.

you really can't avoid the question of preservation.

Various methods are available, depending not only on your own preferences and the use you'll be making of the herbs, but above all on the substances contained in them. The methods themselves are briefly explained in the rest of this chapter; the method of choice for each plant is given under its profile (see page 34 onwards).

You can tell when the herbs are completely dry because the stems will be brittle. They'll snap easily rather than bending, and the leaves can easily be crumbled into fragments.

The time required for drying will vary from a few days to a few weeks. However, once your herbs have dried, it's a simple job to separate the crumbly leaves from the stems. You can then store them in dark-glass containers with stoppers, always making sure that you label them properly.

Freezing mixtures of herbs in ice-cube trays makes handy portions.

In all cases, it's important that the herbs aren't exposed either to direct sunlight or to temperatures above 110°F (42°C); if you dry them gently, the herbs will keep their valuable contents largely intact. Only a few ingredients can tolerate temperatures up to 150°F (65°C).

The same applies to roots, as well, though in this case it's better to use an oven or some

Strictly speaking tea is an infusion, used not so much to preserve as to 'take' various flavouring and active agents from the fresh or dried drug in liquid form.

Depending on the intensity of the starting material, you take 1–2 teaspoons of dry matter, pour over a scant half pint (¼ litre) of boiling water and let it all stand for 10 minutes.

If you're using fresh herbs, take 6–8 times the amount and ideally bring it to the boil briefly before you leave it to stand.

Roots are usually covered with cold water, then brought briefly to the boil.

Labiates in particular will yield up valuable substances when steeped in oil or vinegar.

similar appliance to help dry them. If they don't dry quickly enough, they can very easily start to rot, and they're vulnerable to pests as well.

On the other hand, you shouldn't turn the heat up too high either — on no account should the oven temperature be allowed to rise above 110–120°F (40–50°C).

To make the roots dry more easily, split the thick ones; you can also put a cord through the split to hang them up for drying. The sun can help a bit with the

drying, and once the roots are completely dry and brittle, you can crush them up and put them into containers.

Freezing

In many cases freezing is the gentlest method to use. This applies particularly to parsley and dill; from what we've heard, they lose a lot of their properties when dried. Lemon balm and peppermint, on the other hand, have proved less suitable for freezing.

After your herbs have been harvested, then the quicker you can get them into the freezer, the better. The best way to do this is to put them in plastic tubs or bags; once they're frozen it's often easy to crumble them up into small pieces.

An old trick is to freeze small quantities of herbs with a little water in ice-cube trays: that way, you can easily add the resulting portions to salads or sauces. Of course, you can also make up your own herb mixtures for this.

Steeping herbs in vinegar or oil

Dill, tarragon and basil vinegars are all well known, but lemon balm and other herbs can also give vinegar an interesting savour. Basil, like marjoram, thyme, sage and other labiates, yields its flavour readily to vegetable oils.

The procedure is a simple one: just put the herbs in a bottle, and cover them completely with the liquid.

For this job you should splash out on a really good-quality wine or fruit vinegar, or a cold-pressed (olive) oil. Only a quality product can give your herb extract its due.

Whole portions of the plant look attractive in vinegar, but if you're infusing your herbs in vinegar, you should cut them into small pieces. That way they'll yield their ingredients more effectively.

Use a translucent container for the oil, and stand it in the sun. Give the whole thing a good shake several times, and after about three weeks most of the ingredients from the herbs will have passed into the vinegar or the oil. You must strain the oil before use; press out the residue in the sieve thoroughly so you lose as little as possible.

Herb salt

Here is yet another way to make herbs last. Herb salt is particularly effective with many of the traditional native seasonings. Chop them as finely as possible, and add about a quarter by weight of salt (i.e. one part salt to four of herbs).

Parsley, dill and tarragon are popular candidates for this treatment, but be more careful with labiates (e.g. marjoram or savory). Members of the onion family aren't suitable for this method of preservation. On the other hand it's often a good idea to mince up some sweet pepper or spicy root of parsnip, celeriac or lovage, and add it to the herb and salt mixture.

33

The most popular culinary herb

Parsley
(Petroselinum crispum)

Botany: This popular culinary herb came from the south-east Mediterranean. It develops fleshy roots, and it's biennial, so you must wait until May of its second year before you see the umbelliferous heads of the small flowers appear from the leaf rosettes. Parsley grows up to 4 ft (1.2 m) tall. Consumers are interested only in the foliage, which lasts for about 14 months. If you want to collect the seed, leave the plants until flowering has finished.

Curly parsley (e.g. 'Moss Curled') is preferred for its appearance, and makes an excellent garnish. But the plain-leaved French or Italian varieties have a stronger flavour and are far hardier.

Position: Parsley prefers humus- and nutrient-rich soil, so it thrives in the vegetable patch. It will tolerate relatively acid peaty soils as well as semi-shaded situations.

Cultivation: From late March onwards, you can sow parsley directly out of doors, in drills about 12 in (30 cm) apart (if you wish, soak the seeds in hot water first). Parsley germinates quickly in warm soil: you can help by pouring boiling water along the drills and covering the soil two weeks before sowing.

Cover the seeds with no more than ½ in (1 cm) of soil and keep them moist until they germinate, without letting the soil turn to mud. Thin later to 6 in (15 cm) apart.

Like many umbellifers, parsley needs a long germination period (21 days, or more in cold weather). It's vulnerable at this time, so it's a good idea to sow the seed in pans or pots first. Prick out the seedlings once before planting the strong young herbs outside in May.

Parsley should not be grown repeatedly in the same place. If it is, various forms of damage will appear, so don't put it back on the same site for another three or four years. If you still have trouble growing parsley from seed, try sowing in June or July. Summer temperatures produce the ideal conditions for germination, but you mustn't forget to keep the seed damp.

Parsley won't tolerate fresh animal manure, but you can apply organic fertilisers when planting out. If you take a full harvest from the plants, then after each cut it's a good idea to give 2–3 small handfuls of an organic complete fertiliser (e.g. blood-fish-and-bone) per square yard/metre.

Parsley can be grown in the greenhouse over the winter. To do this, sow seed direct in August or plant seedlings in

With Hamburg parsley you harvest the whitish roots from the ground in the autumn (the yield is bigger in the second year). They're particularly suitable as a flavouring in soup, for raw salads, or as a vegetable rather like celeriac. What you don't use at once you bury in sand, and store in a cool room.

If you leave the growing point on the root vegetable, you can force it into growth in winter as well. That way you can have parsley leaves on your window-sill.

34

Despite this, however, parsley is used almost exclusively as a seasoning. There are innumerable ways to use it for salads, soups, sauces, potatoes and other vegetables, as well as all sorts of meat.

In spite of this versatility, it's better not to overuse parsley: like so many good things, it can be harmful in excess, especially during pregnancy.

Left *Curly parsley varieties make a prettier garnish, but plain-leaved ones are more nutritious.*

Below *Hamburg parsley can be brought into growth on the windowsill in winter.*

September at the latest. Rows should be rather closer together, at 8 in (20 cm).

Harvest and preservation:
You can take fresh leaves continually from May until well into winter, when it's a good idea to cloche the plants so that they're protected from the worst of the frost and snow.

In the second spring you can continue harvesting until the flowers develop. If you want to collect seed, you can let some plants flower.

If you've sown direct in the open, you may be able to start a full harvest as early as May, and carry on cutting successively every 6 weeks.

Parsley shouldn't be cooked with food: serve it as fresh and as raw as possible, or it loses too much of its flavour. If it has to be preserved, it's one of the few herbs you can dry in the oven. Keep the door open and don't let the temperature go over 195°F (90°C).

Two other common preservation methods are freezing and salting.

Active agents and application: As well as essential oils, the leaves contain large amounts of vitamin C, which is what makes parsley valuable. It also aids digestion, cleanses the blood, and acts as a diuretic and a decongestant.

Tasty foliage from umbellifers

Chervil
(Antbriscus cerefolium)

Botany: This annual plant originated in south-east Europe. Inflorescences appear between May and August, growing up to 28 in (70 cm) tall.

Position: Freshly dug, friable garden soils in semi-shade.

Cultivation: Chervil is sown out of doors from March to July, broadcast or in drills 6 in (15 cm) apart. Like parsley it needs light and time to germinate, and has plain- and curly-leaved varieties. If it's grown as an early catch crop in the vegetable patch, don't use fertiliser. You can apply two small handfuls of organic complete fertiliser per square yard/metre straight after cutting, or while it's sprouting the second time if necessary. Keep down the weeds, and cut off any flowers.

Harvest and preservation: You can cut the shoots after just 5 weeks, but think about further harvests (after another 4 weeks), and don't damage the heart of the plant. Don't cook chervil leaves: add them raw. Freezing and salting preserve the flavour better than slow drying.

Active agents and application: essential oils, bitter principles and vitamin C act together to improve the metabolism and cleanse the blood.

The sweetish aromatic flavour goes best with green salad, tomatoes, savoury spreads, soups or lamb.

Lovage
(Levisticum officinale)

Botany: This herbaceous perennial can grow to over 6 ft (around 2 m). It came into our latitudes through the Middle East and southern Europe. The umbels of yellow flowers appear from June through until August.

Position: The soil should be fresh and full of humus, deep, moist and nutrient-rich.

Cultivation: Sow lovage under glass from February onwards, or straight outside from May. It's easier to divide the roots and get specimens which are already young plants; plant them in April or September/October.

One plant per household is sufficient (see picture on page 26). Give lovage a handful of organic fertiliser in spring, or after a heavy harvest.

If you plan to harvest the roots, remove the flowers as they start to open.

Harvest and preservation: You can pick the foliage continually, but it's better picked before flowering if possible. Preserve it by drying, freezing, or steeping in vinegar or oil.

The spicy-sweet chervil can be picked after only five weeks.

The roots are used, too. Dig them up in their second autumn, wash them, chop them finely, and grind them when they've dried.

Active agents and application: Besides essential oils, lovage contains resin, starch and various acids. You can cook small quantities of tender leaves (and roots) with soups, sauces, casseroles and meat dishes: this produces a pleasant flavour, and has a digestive and diuretic effect. Tea made from the roots is considered a good remedy for stomach complaints. However, pregnant women should go easy with this seasoning.

Celery
(Apium graveolens)

Botany: The wild form blooms in its second spring, but celery is cultivated only as an annual plant. The herb variety is grown for its leaves; other varieties are grown for their long stems (blanched celery) or their roots (celeriac, turnip-rooted celery).

Position: Celery is at home throughout the Old World on salty soils in regions with a mild climate. Garden soil should be sufficiently moist and rich in nutrients.

Cultivation: Sow celery under glass from March. The seed is *photopositive* — it needs light in order to germinate. Prick out, plant in open ground after the frosts in late May. From May you can also sow outdoors in rows 14 in (35 cm) apart, thinning

later to 10 in (25 cm) within the rows.

Celery tolerates a good application of rotted garden compost as fertiliser, and perhaps a fast-acting top-dressing (e.g. liquid fertiliser made from stinging nettles) in June/July.

Harvesting and preservation: Harvest fresh leaves continually from June on, but don't touch the heart. Freeze or dry leaves after the main autumn harvest.

Unlike the varieties grown for their stems or roots, this celery is used only as a seasoning.

Active agents and application: Essential oils, bitter principles and hormones make finely chopped celery leaves an excellent seasoning that acts as a diuretic and stimulates vital energies. Celery goes well with salads, but is better when cooked with soups, potato dishes, casseroles and meat.

The spicy fruits of the umbellifers

Most herbs in this section don't need special treatment with fertiliser. You want them to form seeds, and they get enough encouragement to do this in the lean soil of the herb bed. When they're grown in a vegetable plot there should be an adequate supply of nutrients, if the usual fertiliser has been applied.

Dill
(Anethum graveolens)
Botany: Dill is an annual herb from the Near East. While it's flowering (i.e from July to September), it can reach up to 4 ft (1.2 m) in height. the so-called tetraploid varieties of dill are characterised by thicker foliage.

Position: The soil should be fresh, but well-drained and humus-rich; dill is a calcicole (i.e. a lime-lover). Sunny situations sheltered from the wind are also ideal.

Cultivation: Dill can be sown very shallowly out of doors from April till July, with 8 in (20 cm) between rows. You can moisten the seeds first to encourage germination. You can transplant seedlings started under glass, but only if their root balls remain intact.

Dill won't tolerate animal manure or frost. It thrives in mixed cultivation with carrots or cucumbers, but if it's grown in the vegetable plot do rotate it with other umbellifers. If you want to save seed from dill or fennel, don't grow them near each other; the resulting seed will be a hybrid.

Harvest and preservation: You can cut the feathery, tender foliage continually for salads. Let the seeds ripen on the plant until they turn pale brown, but gather the umbels before the seeds drop out, early on a dry morning.

Active agents and application: The high levels of essential oils help to strengthen and calm the stomach. Tea made from dill seeds is also used for this purpose.

The leaves have an aromatic, slightly bitter flavour, which

You can gather the leaves as well as the seeds from the tender dill plants.

makes them an excellent complement to vegetables, salads, white sauces, and meat and fish dishes. Don't cook the herb: add it shortly before serving.

Another typical application is in pickling gherkins. Freeze dill or steep it (in vinegar or oil) to preserve its flavour.

Caraway
(Carum carvi)

Botany: Caraway is a native of Europe and Asia, growing up to 4 ft (1.2 m) when the inflorescences form — i.e. from the May of its second year.

Position: Caraway grows wild in damp meadows, in semi-shade. It needs deep, chalky soil to develop as well as possible.

Cultivation: Caraway needs light in order to germinate. Sow it very shallowly out of doors between April and July. The rows should be 12 in (30 cm) apart, and the soil must be kept moist. It may need protection in a hard winter.

Harvest and application: The seeds turn brown as they ripen (from the July of the second year), by which time you should harvest them.

Cut off the umbels and leave them to dry in a well-ventilated location, then knock out the single, crescent-shaped fruits. When these are completely dry, you should store them in an airtight container.

You can use the young leaves as a seasoning during the plant's first year.

You can hardly fail to notice the relationship between caraway (left) and coriander (below left). Both of these herbs can be used to aid digestion.

Active agents and application: The essential oils help with stomach and intestinal complaints, and counter flatulence. Caraway is a tried-and-tested ingredient in all foods that are hard to digest such as vegetables, meat or bread. Caraway tea can achieve the same effects.

Coriander
(Coriandrum sativum)

Botany: This annual plant comes from the Mediterranean area. It flowers from June onwards with little whitish-pink umbels, reaching a height of up to 28 in (70 cm).

Position: Warm and sunny sites on free-draining, chalky soil.

Cultivation: Sow direct outside from April onwards, ½–¾ in (1–2 cm) deep, in drills 12 in (30 cm) apar;, thin later to 6 in (15 cm) within rows. This plant requires little attention beyond occasional loosening of the soil (remove unwanted wild plants in the process). Coriander grows quickly to the flowering stage.

Harvest and preservation: Harvest the multiple fruits on an overcast day in August, before the seeds ripen fully and drop to the ground by themselves. Hang up the umbels head-down. The round seeds are in two halves; once they're completely dry and pale brown, knock them out and store them in an airtight container.

You can add young shoot-tips to salads and other uncooked dishes as a seasoning.

Active agents and application: The essential oils, like those of caraway, are appetite-stimulating and antispasmodic, but they taste rather fresher. Coriander, with its orangy flavour, makes a good spice for vegetables, for curry sauces, for use in preserving, and for bread and cakes.

Anise
(Pimpinella anisum)

Botany: This frost-tender seasoning herb from the eastern Mediterranean comes into flower from July onwards, growing up to 32 in (80 cm) tall. The strains that flourish in our climate have less flavour than their southern cousins.

Position: Anise is planted and grown much like coriander. It prefers warm and sunny sites on well-drained, chalky subsoil. If there isn't enough warmth, the fruits don't ripen.

Cultivation: Sow directly outside from April onwards, about 1 in (2-3 cm) deep in drills 10 in (25 cm) apart, thinning out to 6 in (15 cm) within rows. Germination is slow. Hoe occasionally.

Harvest and preservation: The first fruits ripen from August onwards. Hang the seed-

heads up somewhere airy, knock out the seeds once they have dried, and store them in an airtight container.

Active agents and application: The essential oil in anise promotes digestion, counters flatulence and helps phlegm to loosen. A tea made from the seeds can alleviate a catarrhal cough. As a seasoning, anise has a typical sweetish flavour. Use it cautiously with vegetables such as red cabbage or beetroot, and with baked foods or liqueurs.

Fennel
(Foeniculum vulgare)

Botany: Originally from the Mediterranean region, this perennial seasoning herb can overwinter farther north, but will need protection in hard

winters. Inflorescences form from July in the second year, reaching over 5½ ft (1.6 m).

Unlike Florence fennel, which is grown for its 'bulbs', the herb fennel is of interest for its leaves and seeds.

Position: Fennel needs a site offering Mediterranean warmth, with full sun and good drainage. It also requires a deep, chalky and above all nutrient-rich subsoil.

Cultivation: Sow very shallow outside from April on, in rows 8-10 in (20-25 cm) apart. Then transplant the following year, to a spacing of approximately 20 × 20 in (50 × 50 cm).

Rotted garden compost or animal manure speeds up development. Cut hard back before overwintering, and in

colder areas cover the crowns with a heavy mulch to protect them from frost.

The plants take up a relatively large amount of space; this is why people with large gardens tend to prefer fennel.

Harvest and preservation: From August of the second year, the fruits show they're ripe by turning brown. They don't all ripen at once, so you must

Left *Anise, coriander and caraway (from left to right) must all be harvested at the right moment, before their seeds drop out.*

Below *Hoverflies are interested in the fennel's flowers, which they help to pollinate, so ensuring seed.*

either pick the ripe ones in several batches, or hang up entire umbels to ripen and dry out. Afterwards, knock them out over a newspaper or a bit of cloth and store in an airtight container.

Active agents and application: The essential oils in fennel stimulate the stomach and relax spasms, as well as combating flatulence. A tea made with the seeds helps with coughs, and acts as a tranquilliser.

With its sweetish-spicy taste, fennel seed adds an interesting and unusual flavour to any baked food. Young shoots used as a fresh seasoning go nicely with salads, sauces, soups and vegetables.

Aromatic labiates

Savory
(Satureja species)

Botany: Two species of savory are used as herbs: the annual summer savory *(S. hortensis)* and the perennial subshrub winter savory *(S. montana)*. Both come from the Mediterranean, and grow no higher than 16–20 in (40–50 cm).

Winter savory flowers first, from June onwards; the white blossom makes good 'pasture' for bees. Annual savory has purplish-tinged leaves and stems, and lilac flowers.

Position: Ideal for the annual species are light, humus-rich, chalky garden soils in the sunshine. Winter savory is if anything even less demanding, making do with a warm spot in the rock garden.

Cultivation: Both savory species need light to germinate, so don't cover the seed. They can be sown outdoors from April to May. It may be worth starting off seedlings of the annual species under glass from March onwards, planting out in late April.

Savory flourishes in mixed cultivation in the vegetable plot, preferably with beans. If you grow savory on its own, leave

Unlike the annual summer savory, winter savory can get to be several years old.

approximately 10 in (25 cm) between rows.

You can apply a little hoof-and-horn after a full-scale harvest, and when you cut back the subshrub after flowering or overwintering. In very cold areas it's advisable to protect winter savory with brushwood for overwintering. The annual species is frost tender.

Harvest and preservation: Pick leaves and shoot-tips at any time. The best time for the main harvest is before the plants start flowering. Afterwards you can dry the herb well, but also steep it in oil or freeze it instead.

Active agents and application: Essential oils, tannins and bitter principles are resposible for its digestive and stimulant characteristics.

Savory's close link with beans is partly on account of its anti-flatulent effect, but also because of its thyme-like, peppery taste — rather more pronounced in the case of winter savory. The herb goes well with many other dishes too. The tea can also be taken for coughs.

Basil
(Ocimum basilicum)

Botany: This tender annual herb from the Orient comes into flower from July on. There are varieties with purple leaves and with different-sized ones (the smaller leaves are richer in content), and many wild and decorative forms named according to their flavour or leaf form (e.g. dwarf, lemon, curly basil).

For many dishes, you can't do without the powerful aroma of basil.

Position: A warm and sunny site out of the wind, and humus-rich, friable soil.

Cultivation: Sow in warmth under glass from the end of March. The seeds need light (so don't cover them) and lots of moisture to germinate; they turn blue as they absorb water.

After all danger of frost is past, you can plant out at a spacing of 6 × 6 in (15 × 15 cm), but since basil is sensitive to cold and damp, and snails enjoy eating it too, you can grow it on in the greenhouse, or in a window-box or conservatory.

An application of fertiliser will promote leaf development, but basil can't tolerate manure.

Harvest and preservation: As soon as the plants are strong enough, you can pick the tips of shoots continually — this helps the plant to develop a bushy habit. Basil's aroma is strongest just before it flowers, so this is the best time for the main harvest, though its leaves lose much of their flavour when preserved.

Freezing and steeping in vinegar or oil conserve more flavour than drying. Tear up fresh leaves very small and add just before serving; don't cook with foods.

Active agents and application: While still in the ground, basil is said to deter flies. The essential oils, mucilages and tannins ensure a calming effect, which can help with stomach upsets and lack of appetite. The tea helps with catarrhal coughs.

Normally this herb has a spicy-sweet flavour, but lemon- or camphor-like varieties also exist. It can be used as the main seasoning with salads (especially tomatoes) and sauces, and with meat dishes containing wine and garlic.

Sweet marjoram
(Origanum majorana)

Botany: This herb, an annual here, is from the Mediterranean. It flowers between June and September, growing up to 20 in (50 cm) tall. It has a unique and peculiarly sweet aroma. The buds are round and green, and their shape gives it the alternative name knotted marjoram.

Position: It prefers a warm, sunny site on well-drained, chalky, humus-rich subsoil.

Cultivation: From March onwards, raise the seeds (but don't cover them — they need light) on the window-sill in constant moisture. The seedlings need warmth, so only when all risk of frost is past should you plant them outside, at a spacing of 10 × 6 in (25 × 15 cm).

Harvest and preservation: Take leaves and young shoots at any time for fresh consumption. The main harvest is when the flowers are just in bud (from July); you may get another

Above *Wild marjoram will grow even out in a meadow, but the ground must be warm and free-draining.*

Left *Gather sweet marjoram just before the flower buds open.*

harvest in the autumn. The leaves can be dried, frozen or steeped in oil to preserve them.

Active agents and application: The effect of the essential oils, tannins and bitter principles is described as calming, decongestant and appetite-stimulating. Correspondingly, a tea helps in cases of digestive complaints and flatulence.

The herb's spicy-sweet aroma has proved its worth with potatoes and in casseroles, with meat, game and poultry, and as a sausage ingredient.

Wild marjoram
(Origanum vulgare)

Botany: This herbaceous perennial is native to Britain, southern Europe and the Near East, but can also be found nowadays in warm mountainous regions of Europe. Marjoram reaches a height of up to 40 in (1 m) and blooms from July to September, attracting numerous insects to its flowers. A well-tried variety is *O. v.* 'Compactum', and a particularly decorative one is golden marjoram (*O. v.* 'Aureum').

Position: Originally grown on poor, chalky meadowland, it does admittedly need a well-drained position, but is otherwise pretty undemanding.

Cultivation: Sow the seeds under glass (don't cover them) from March onwards, and plant out in late April, spacing 10 × 10 in (25 × 25 cm) apart. You can dig in well-rotted garden compost or animal manure beforehand. As it spreads by means of shallow roots running from a central crown, it's easy to propagate by division. One fully grown specimen is enough.

After the main harvest, you may apply well-rotted garden compost or other organic fertiliser, but only until August. Only very occasionally will protection against frost be needed; a greater danger is waterlogging.

Harvest and preservation: Take single leaves and shoot-tips as a fresh ingredient at any time. For the main harvest, you should ideally cut non-woody shoots between July and September. To preserve them you can dry them, freeze them or steep them in oil.

Active agents and application: Tannins and bitter principles, along with the essential oils, stimulate bile production and loosen catarrh. The tea is administered for coughs and certain stomach complaints. The flavour, rather similar to that of thyme, is typical of Italian cuisine (pizza, tomato sauce etc.), and especially enhances fatty meat and vegetable dishes.

Thyme
(Thymus species)

Botany: Common thyme (*T. vulgaris*) is an evergreen sub-shrub from the western Mediterranean; it blooms from May onwards, and grows up to 16 in (40 cm). Another popular culinary thyme is *T.* × *citriodorus*, with its lemon-scented leaves, looser growth habit and later flowering period; though just as

The numerous species and varieties of thyme also mean you can use it to artistic effect.

popular with bees, it is slightly less hardy than *T. vulgaris*.

Creeping thyme *(T. serpyllum)* is a very low-growing alpine that forms carpets of flowers in various shades of pinky purple, creating an attractive patchwork. There are many other decorative and useful species and varieties.

Position: Dry, sunny sites on chalky and free-draining soils. In the garden, the rock garden is often ideal, or, for lemon thyme, the herbaceous border.

Cultivation: All the species mentioned should be grown in the same way. Sow under glass from March on; plant out from May at a spacing of 8 × 8 in (20 × 20 cm). You can also propagate thyme from April onwards using non-woody cuttings, or by layering in summer.

Thyme is vulnerable to waterlogging, but should be watered occasionally during a persistent dry spell. It doesn't tolerate manure at all well; at best, apply some fertiliser in the form of well-rotted garden compost and hoof-and-horn after you've cut it for harvest. Thyme is sensitive to frost, you shouldn't continue to transplant it in the autumn; in harsher situations, it's a good idea to cover it against the frost. After four years the plants become very woody.

Harvest and preservation: Cut shoot-tips at any time for use as a fresh ingredient. For the main harvest (between May and August), cut back to 3–4 in (8–10 cm) above the ground, ideally in the early afternoon.

Dry the shoots in the shade and pick off the leaves before putting them in a container.

Active agents and application: Essential oils, tannins and bitter principles have a digestive, anti-spasmodic, decongestant and disinfectant effect. For coughs, bronchitis or stomach complaints, take a cup of the tea (or gargle with it), or take a bath. As a seasoning, thyme goes with soups, sauces and stuffings, as well as with meat and vegetable dishes flavoured with lots of onions and wine.

Sage
(Salvia officinalis)

Botany: This evergreen subshrub with its grey-green leaves comes from the Mediterranean. It grows to 28 in (70 cm), and produces blue labiate flowers in June and July. There are many related ornamental forms.

Position: A warm and sunny spot on dry, chalky subsoil; in our climate, choose a situation sheltered from the wind; sage is sensitive to cold and damp.

Cultivation: Sow under glass in March or outside from April; or propagate by division in April/ May or by cuttings the summer. The final spacing of seedlings is 12 × 12 in (30 × 30 cm). As a rule, one plant is enough.

Sage grows happily in mixed cultivation with herbs, vegetables and herbaceous perennials, and even tolerates applications of rotted manure. In severe winters, mulch thickly round the base of the plant; while temperatures remain low, cover the top

growth with netting, plastic sheeting or brushwood . In spring, cut the shoots back to about 4 in (10 cm) long.

Harvest and preservation: Young leaves from non-woody shoots can be picked at any time, preferably late on a sunny afternoon. If you want to keep the leaves , dry them in the shade and store them in closed, lightproof, airtight containers, or steep them in oil or vinegar.

Active agents and application: Essential oils combine with tannins and bitter principles to achieve a digestive, but above all an anti-inflammatory and disinfectant effect. Sage tea is a well-tried remedy in cases of coughs and throat inflammations, but shouldn't be taken for longer periods of time.

Above *With rosemary it's best to take the tips of non-woody shoots.*

Left *Sage's attractive flowers make it an interesting plant for the herbaceous border.*

As a seasoning, sage is added sparingly to meat, fish and poultry, as well as to hearty vegetable dishes.

Rosemary
(Rosmarinus officinalis)

Botany: Rosemary is an evergreen up to 5 ft (1.5 m) tall — one of the shrubs which grow near the shores of the Mediterranean. It has needle-like leaves, and survives all but the severest winters, particularly in front of a south-facing wall.

Position: Free-draining and humus-rich soils in a warm, sunny spot. Rosemary makes a good container plant, and then has the added advantage that it can be moved under cover in really cold weather.

Cultivation: The best way to propagate is by cuttings (June–August), but it's also possible to sow seed under glass from March onwards. Rooted plants can be planted out from April onwards, at a spacing of 16 × 16 in (40 × 40 cm), though one plant per household is enough.

From late summer onwards, only water sparingly so that the wood can ripen. If your garden is a cold one, or the winter is particularly hard, it's best to put rosemary into a container and store it in a conservatory or greenhouse. Cut out any dead shoots in the spring.

Harvest and preservation: You can pick 4–6-in (10–15-cm) long non-woody shoot tips continually until August, if possible on sunny days. When they're dried and stripped from the stalk, the leaves lose more of their savour than if frozen or steeped in vinegar or oil.

Active agents and application: The essential oils promote circulation and digestion; a tea or bath from the leaves also strengthens the nerves. Rosemary has a camphoric, rather bitter and refreshing aroma that goes with various sauces, game, poultry and lamb. Anyone who is pregnant should go easy on this seasoning.

To obtain lavender's active agents, you must rob the plant of its flowers.

Lavender
(Lavandula angustifolia)

Botany: This silvery-grey evergreen subshrub originates in the western Mediterranean, and reaches heights of up to 32 in (80 cm); it's especially typical of southern France. In July and August, lavender's flowers give off the scent that we all know so well. A close relative is *L. latifolia*.

Position: The scents develop best if lavender is grown on chalky, free-draining soils in a sunny situation. It also has a firm place in the flower-bed, particularly as a partner to roses.

Cultivation: You can sow seed under glass in March/April, but most people propagate lavender by cuttings taken in spring. You can also divide old clumps in May or September, replanting at a spacing of 16 × 16 in (40 × 40 cm). When grown in the flower-bed, lavender will tolerate the application of well-rotted garden compost as a fertiliser, but a more powerful fragrance develops if it's grown under poorer conditions.

Cut back lightly after flowering, and maybe provide some protective covering against frost so as to ensure that your lavender will flourish.

Harvest and preservation: For small-scale use, you can keep cutting shoot-tips continually, but as the fragrance is mainly carried by the flowers, you should undertake the main harvest just before they open. Dry the flower spikes, then take the individual flowers off the stalks, though you can also freeze the shoot-tips or steep them in oil.

Active agents and application: The essential oils extend a calming influence; the scent alone is enough. They also promote the circulation, an effect achieved both by a tea (mostly in mixtures) and by a herbal bath.

>  **Herbal bath:** Bring 2 oz lavender to the boil in 2 pt water (50 g in 1 litre), strain, and add the liquid to the bath water.

For seasoning you can add the shoot-tips sparingly to sauces, casseroles and fish dishes.

And finally, lavender flowers have long been a fixed element in scented pillows and sachets for household linen and wardrobes. One of their many uses is to keep moths out of clothes.

Hyssop
(Hyssopus officinalis)

Botany: From June onwards, this subshrub from the Mediterranean region blooms in shades of blue, and in whitish and pink tones too. It's a valuable feeding ground for bees, reaching heights of up to 2 ft (60 cm).

Position: In order to thrive, hyssop needs lots of sun, as well as humus-rich, chalky, free-draining soil. Because of its attractive flowers, it is often grown in flower-beds where the soil has the same qualities.

Cultivation: You can sow the seeds under glass from March, or outdoors from April onwards (don't cover them with the soil). It's simpler to divide existing clumps in the spring or autumn,

replanting them at a spacing of 12 × 10 in (30 × 25 cm). You can also take cuttings from the non-woody shoots.

Hyssop tolerates a fertiliser application of well-rotted garden compost. After flowering, cut it back to 3–4 in (8–10 cm) above the ground. If necessary, cover the plants up a little for the winter.

Harvest and preservation: The leaves and shoot-tips can be picked continually. Just before flowering, you may cut the plant back hard by about three-quarters for the main harvest; with older plants, you can do

this again in September.

You can dry hyssop gently to preserve it, but it's better to freeze it or steep it in oil.

Active agents and application: Hyssop's essential oils and tannins have anti-spasmodic and digestive effects, and as a tea it work as an expectorant for chesty coughs.

Used sparingly as a seasoning, hyssop goes with salads and soups, with beans, various roasts and fish.

If you allow hyssop to flower, it will provide a feast for bees and many other insects.

Refreshing labiates

Lemon balm
(Melissa officinalis)

Botany: This herbaceous perennial comes from the eastern Mediterranean and the Near East, and grows up to 4 ft (1.2 m) tall. Small white labiate flowers appear in July/August. The leaves have an intense aroma of lemon.

Position: A warm and sunny spot: mildew takes hold in a damp microclimate. Soil should be humus-rich and friable.

Cultivation: Seed can be sown under glass from March on, but germination is slow, needing light and warmth as well as moisture. It's easier to divide and plant clumps outside from May on. You can also propagate by cuttings. One plant per household is enough; occupying up 20 × 20 in (50 × 50 cm).

To encourage the fragrant leaves, give the clump an application of rotted manure in spring. After the full harvest, one or two handfuls of hoof-and-horn ensure strong new growth. To prolong the harvest season, cut the shoots back before flowering. If flowers are left on the plant, it will self-seed so enthusiastically that you may begin to regard it as a weed.

Harvest and preservation: Gather shoot-tips and leaves continually for fresh use. For the main harvest, cut shoots down to 3-4 in (8-10 cm) on overcast days before flowering starts (around 24 June). Afterwards, strip the leaves from the stalk.

The dried leaves lose much of their lemony flavour. It's better to steep them in oil or else freeze them.

Active agents and application: The essential oils in the leaves strengthen the nerves, and (curiously) are both calming and invigorating. They also reduce irritation and have an antispasmodic action. A tea or a bath is equally helpful.

As a refreshing seasoning, lemon balm is best with salads and sauces, fish and poultry.

Peppermint
(Mentha × piperita)

Botany: The well-known tea herb is a hybrid of three wild species — *M. longifolia, M. suareolens* and *M. aquatica* — all of them native to Europe and Asia. The result is that this herbaceous perennial can only

On fresh, nutrient-rich soils, lemon balm grows to form luxuriant, sweet-smelling bushes.

be propagated vegetatively. It flowers from July onwards; depending on variety, and grows up to about 32 in (80 cm) tall.

The related species *M. spicata* supplies the well-known spearmint flavour. A subspecies of this, *M. s. crispa*, has curly-edged leaves.

Position: Peppermint likes a fairly fresh, moist site, but won't tolerate waterlogging. It prefers humus-rich soil in a sunny situation, but will also grow in semi-shaded sites or bogland.

Cultivation: Propagation is vegetative, mainly by layering the creeping underground stems about 4-6 in (10-15 cm) deep in the spring or (better) in the autumn. If you take tip cuttings between May and July, they will root in 6-8 weeks in a moist growing medium.

Peppermint tends to spread like a weed, so you should install a barrier around the site where you want to grow it, right down to about 6 in (15 cm) below the surface.

You can apply an organic fertiliser such as rotted animal manure in spring or after the harvest, but too much nitrogen and damp can lead to peppermint rust — a fungal disease. Affected plants must be cut hard back and all fallen leaves should be removed.

Harvest and preservation: You can cut smaller quantities for seasoning continually. For

The look and scent of peppermint make it a good garnish for sophisticated drinks.

Restricting the roots down to a depth of 6 in (15 cm) stops peppermint running wild.

the main harvest, cut the herb — which should be dry — hand-high above the ground when the flower buds appear; this is normally done in July, and possibly again in September. Strip the leaves from the stalk, and dry them in the shade or freeze them (the latter will keep the aroma better).

Active agents and application: The essential oil has an anti-spasmodic and cooling-analgesic action; the tea can be drunk as a remedy for colds and nausea, though not by people with stomach ulcers. Also, small children shouldn't take the tea regularly over a long period.

With foods, peppermint is added only in small quantities; avoid mixing it with other seasonings as far as possible. It goes with soups and sauces, vegetables and raw dishes, but also with sweet foods or refreshing drinks. The scent has a stimulating effect in cases of mental exhaustion.

A savoury garnish

Chives
(Allium schoenoprasum)

Botany: This plant belongs to the lily family, and to the same genus as onions and garlic. Like them, it survives the winter by means of underground bulbs. It has spread in the wild, and now grows throughout the temperate northern hemisphere. The pink to lilac flowers develop from as early as May, reaching a height of just 12 in (30 cm).

Position: Chalky and humus-rich meadows in the sunshine are home to this grass-like relative of the onion, but it can also be grown quite successfully in the semi-shade of a woodland floor.

Cultivation: In March/April, sow direct into open ground or a garden frame, either station-sown or evenly, in rows spaced 12 in (30 cm) apart. For winter cultivation, sow in August as well. You could also start it off under glass from February onwards. Beware — the seeds only remain viable for a year!

It's also possible to divide up old clumps in spring or autumn; planting them out again at a spacing of 10 × 10 in (25 × 25 cm). Remove the first flowers until the roots have grown properly, to concentrate the plant's strength on vegetative development.

On established plants, remove the flower heads before they unfold to improve leaf development. If the plants are close together, there's less room for weeds to get established, but the plants will also be more vulnerable to fungal diseases.

Chives need plenty of water in dry weather. In spring, you might like to work in about 2–3 small handfuls of organic fertiliser per square yard/metre, but note that they are decidedly intolerant of fresh manure or unrotted garden compost.

If you want to harvest chives in winter as well, dig the root

If you want a good harvest, you really shouldn't let chives come into flower at all.

balls out between October and February, and let them freeze through once. This freezing is the stimulates the tiny bulbs to send up shoots again after they've died back in autumn. Alternatively, you can break the buds' dormancy by soaking the root balls in warm water at 100°F (38°C) for several hours. Drying them out at 68-77°F (20-25°C) has the same effect.

Afterwards, set the plants in pots or boxes on the window-sill or in the greenhouse and force them at a room temperature of 68°F (20°C), until they are ready for cutting again.

Garlic or Chinese chives *(Allium tuberosum)* have the edible leaves of chives and (in a mild form) the flavour of garlic. They can be grown as annuals or sown from seed, but don't cut much the first year; after this treat them as perennials and divide them, or resow if you prefer. They grow to 20 in (50 cm). Sow from April onwards, in rows 12 in (30 cm) apart; start cutting the spicy leaves in June.

Harvest and preservation: From April onwards there's enough foliage for you to cut it continually for the kitchen. If you cut the flowers back before they bloom, you make harvesting easier later on, as the hard flower stems aren't suitable for consumption. Under favourable

conditions you can get four full harvests a year.

Chives should preferably be used fresh; they can be frozen, but other methods of preservation are out of the question.

Active agents and application: The essential oils contained in chives have the effects of reducing high blood-pressure and stimulating the digestion. Above all, the high vitamin C content is valuable, especially when chives are used to enrich

Garlic chives combine a mild garlic flavour with the simplicity of harvesting leaves.

the winter menu. Chives should never be cooked; only use them raw. Their mild oniony flavour makes them suitable for sandwich fillings (mixed, for example, with a low-fat soft cheese such as quark or fromage frais), as well as for all sorts of salads, for soups and for sauces. Chives also make an attractive garnish on potatoes and casseroles.

Strong-flavoured seasonings

Onion-type herbs
(Allium species and varieties)

Botany: The top or tree onion (*A. cepa* Proliferum group) and the European Welsh onion *(A. fistulosum)* are members of the lily family, and both are very closely related to the bulb onion (*A. cepa*). They are natives of western Asia, but nowadays are by and large known only in cultivation.

The European Welsh onion forms numerous 'daughters' around the 'parent' onion; these are only slightly swollen, and you can harvest them virtually all year round, complete with their tubular leaves. They're often used as a substitute for spring onions.

With tree onions, too, the green tubes make popular eating, as do the bulbils — the tiny bulb-like structures that form at the tops of the shoots (hence the name 'top onions').

Position: Sunny sites on humus-rich garden soils are suitable for cultivating these onions; for preference the soil should be dry, and it should never be allowed to become water-logged.

Cultivation: You can start onions off under glass from

February onwards. In March, both tree and European Welsh onions may be sown direct into open ground, either in groups or in rows approximately 8 in (20 cm) apart.

Remember that you should never sow onions in soil that has just received a fresh application of manure. There are a number of reasons for this, but the most important is the consequent danger of infection by onion flies.

The European Welsh onion (Allium fistulosum) forms numerous 'daughters' around the 'parent' onion.

Harvest and preservation: The green tubes of both these onions can be cut continually just as soon as the plants have become strong enough. In the case of cultivars of the European Welsh onion that are grown as perennials, this means they're available virtually all through the year.

In addition to this, the top bulbils of tree onions can be harvested from August onwards.

Active agents and application: The essential oils and the high vitamin-C content promote digestion and act as a diuretic. A tea (made from finely chopped onions, sweetened with honey) can be taken in cases of coughs and influenza.

European Welsh onion, like its close relative the spring onion, makes an excellent addition to salads. Tree-onion bulbils are very good for pickling.

Garlic
(Allium sativum)

Botany: Garlic is yet another member of the lily family, and of the genus *Allium*. Although originally from central Asia, it has long been at home all round the Mediterranean. When the plant flowers (in July and/or August) it can grow up to 3 ft (90 cm) tall.

Position: The subsoil should be deep, rich in humus and nutrients, and not too sandy; the site should be warm and sunny.

Cultivation: Garlic is never grown from seed. In March/April, or also in September/October, you plant the cloves (the natural sections of the bulb) about 1¼-2 in (3-5 cm) deep in the soil. Space the rows 8-10 in (20-25 cm) apart, with the cloves 2-4 in (5-10 cm) apart within the rows.

Always choose your cloves carefully. Don't, for example, use garlic from the supermarket, because this usually comes from a warmer country, and will produce only very weak growth in our more northerly latitudes. Instead, buy your garlic from a garden centre or nursery.

Like the tree onion, garlic produces bulbils from the flower heads, and these can also be used for propagation.

Companion planting with strawberries, and with beetroot and other kinds of vegetable, has proved its worth a thousand times over. Planted under trees, garlic can keep pests off its plant neighbours.

Just under half a small bucket of well-rotted garden compost per square yard/metre (applied, if possible, to the previous crop on the site) promotes the development of strong bulbs. They will be ready to harvest the following summer (when the tops begin to wither).

Harvest and preservation: In summer, when half the foliage has died off, gather the bulbs, plait them into strings, and leave them to dry in the shade.

To preserve them further, you can also steep the cloves in vinegar, oil or salt.

A long but lonely life will be your reward if you eat garlic regularly.

Active agents and application: There is an old saying that you'll have a long but lonely life if you make a habit of eating the very strong-smelling bulbs. They contain large quantities of sulphurous essential oils, not to mention vitamins and even hormones, and these together are responsible for the legendary reputation of this extremely popular culinary herb.

Garlic will generally increase your resistance to disease. It also stimulates the production of bile, and has a relaxing and an antiseptic action. These properties can be put to prophylactic use to combat arteriosclerosis, to reduce high blood pressure and to deal with various stomach or gut problems. It is also believed to combat the symptoms of old age.

There can hardly be a single savoury dish that can't be accompanied by garlic, whether in larger or in smaller quantities. It's entirely a matter of taste.

Horseradish
(Armoracia rusticana)

Botany: This perennial is a member of the Cruciferae (cabbage family), and comes originally from south-eastern Europe and Asia.

The sweet-smelling inflorescences appear in May/June from the second year onwards, reaching a height of up to 4 ft (1.2 m); before that, the leaves will already have grown to an imposing size.

Position: The soil should be moderately heavy, but also deep, rich in humus and nutrients and slightly damp. Horseradish is tolerant of shady situations.

Cultivation: In March/April, you can take root cuttings known as thongs, which are about the thickness of a pencil and 8-12 in (20-30 cm) long. Put them into the ground at an angle so that the pointed base of the cutting tip lies about 6-8 in (15-20 cm) deep (cut the base to an angle if it isn't already pointed). In June remove the weaker shoots, leaving only the strongest of them standing.

If you remove the side shoots of a horseradish, the main roots will develop more strongly.

The tree onion (Allium cepa Proliferum group), also known as the top onion or Egyptian onion, grows tiny bulbils at the tops of the shoots — these too can be eaten, and are delicious pickled.

As well as cultivating the plants in earthed-up rows, you can grow them in mixed cultivation with potatoes. If you plant horseradish under a tree, it helps to keep off diseases.

Three to five plants are ample even for households obsessed with horseradish; for most, one is quite enough! As a rule you remove the flowers.

Horseradish needs generous applications of organic fertiliser. There is also a good way to encourage the development of thick main roots: you dig each plant up, remove the thin side roots from the main roots, and replant it. This is best done in June/July, and preferably on overcast days.

You can use the side roots to raise new plants; but until you plant them, keep them covered up in damp sand. Beware: any side roots that get left behind will start into growth again, then spread and become weeds.

Harvest and preservation: As soon as the foliage has died back in the autumn, you can dig up the roots and keep them covered in damp sand until you need them. Only the thick main roots are suitable for culinary or medicinal purposes. They can be grated for use, either fresh or in dried form.

Active agents and application: The hot flavour is produced by essential oils, including mustard oil, together with glycosides and antibiotically active substances. Horerseradish has an antiseptic, stimulating effect, and contains high levels of vitamin C. You can grate it finely, mix it with the same volume of honey, and take three teaspoonfuls daily to help with kidney complaints or coughs.

As a seasoning, horseradish goes well with fish, meat, sausage and much more. You can also use it as a condiment seasoned with lemon juice and sugar. Cream mixed with grated horseradish is also delicious.

A piquant relationship

The four herbs that follow all belong to the same botanical family, the Compositae, and to the same genus, *Artemisia*.

The more or less tangy, slightly bitter flavour — and the benefits they bring to the digestion — are common to all four of them.

*French tarragon (*Artemisia dracunculus*) is less robust than its Russian relative* A. dracunculoides, *but it's more aromatic.*

Tarragon
(Artemisia dracunculus
and *A. dracunculoides)*

Botany: Tarragon grows wild in Asia and North America. Russian tarragon (*A. dracunculoides*) is more robust than French tarragon (*A. dracunculus*), which isn't fully hardy in severe winters but has a more pleasant, delicate flavour. Both flower in July or August, the French less often. The Russian can grow up to 6 ft (nearly 2 m); the French reaches only 2–3 ft (60–90 cm).

Position: Soils rich in nutrients and humus, fresh but never waterlogged, in a warm situation; tarragon tolerates semi-shade.

Cultivation: Russian tarragon is sown very shallow under glass from March onwards, or from mid-April direct into open ground. Space strong young plants 20 × 20 in (50 × 50 cm) apart. As a rule, though, one plant per household is enough.

French tarragon can be propagated only by vegetative means — e.g. by division of an older clump. You can take root tip cuttings all year round, but only under glass, as the plant dies down in winter.

In spring, or after the main harvest, tarragon likes an application of rotted manure or two handfuls of organic fertiliser. Before winter, French tarragon should be given a protective covering against frost.

Renew the clumps every three or four years.

Harvest and preservation: Take leaves and shoot-tips whenever you wish. Russian tarragon attains its strongest flavour at the bud stage, so it should be cut well back then. French tarragon can stay standing until September.

After drying, pick off the leaves. The flavour is conserved better by freezing or steeping in vinegar or oil.

Active agents and application: Tarragon's essential oils, tannins and bitter principles

Left *With mugwort (Artemisia vulgaris) you only harvest the bud-like shoot tips.*

Right *Wormwood (A. absinthium) is used mainly in conjunction with the fattier foods.*

promote digestion and stimulate bile secretion.

Tarragon is undoubtedly the mildest and most pleasant-tasting herb in the genus *Artemisia*. You can add the finely chopped leaves sparingly to salads, soups and sauces, and to all sorts of meat. It's also very popular for preserves and pickles.

Like dill and lemon balm, tarragon yields a tasty herb vinegar.

Mugwort
(Artemisia vulgaris)

Botany: A summer-green shrub found across Europe, often as a 'weed' on rubble or beside paths and hedges. Mugwort can grow over 6 ft (2 m) tall (though 4 ft/1.2 m is more usual), and displays inconspicuous loose-branching flower clusters from July onwards.

Position: Mugwort isn't very demanding, but it must have a dry and sunny situation on a chalky subsoil.

Cultivation: Starting in March, you can sow the seeds (which need light to germinate) in a garden frame, and from April onwards outside into open

ground. In spring you can take cuttings or split old clumps. As a rule, one plant is enough. To improve the soil apply lime, or fertilisers containing nitrogen.

Harvest and preservation: Use only the tips of shoots in bud; the leaves and opened flowers have a bitter taste. Preserve by drying, salting, or steeping in oil.

Active agents and application: Essential oils and bitter principles stimulate the stomach and gall bladder when mugwort is taken in a tea.

The taste is rather sharp; cook sparingly with foods that are fatty and hard to digest, e.g. duck, goose, oily fish or fatty meat. Don't take it during pregnancy!

59

Wormwood
(Artemisia absinthium)

Botany: A grey-leaved Mediterranean subshrub. The common name, 'wormwood', comes from the same root as 'vermouth', so like the specific name it points to the plant's connection with alcoholic drinks. Wormwood starts flowering in July, and grows to 5 ft (150 cm).

Position: Undemanding; needs free-draining, chalky subsoil, in a dry and sunny situation.

Cultivation: Sow under glass from March onwards, or outside in April or September — or as each household needs only one plant, divide an existing clump or propagate from cuttings. You can give rotted (animal) manure in several applications.

Despite its strong aroma, wormwood makes a good companion plant for currants, and is thought to keep away rust. It can easily run wild.

Harvest and preservation: Take young leaves to use fresh at any time. For the main harvest, cut the shoot-tips while they're in flower, and hang them head-down in the shade to dry.

Active agents and application: Essential oils, bitter principles and tannins stimulate the appetite and have a digestive and antiseptic effect. A tea may be prescribed for stomach and gall-bladder complaints.

As a seasoning, in small quantities, wormwood is best cooked with fatty foods or casseroles.

A few shoots left to stand for some weeks in a clear spirit (e.g. vodka), and if possible mixed with other herbs, produce 'a little something to help the digestion'.

Wormwood is unsuitable for long-term use, and avoid it if you're pregnant.

Southernwood/lad's love
(Artemisia abrotanum)

Botany: A subshrub from the Near East with feathery, needle-like foliage, growing up to 40 in (1 m). In a warm summer it produces tiny, dull-yellow flowers in August/September.

Position: The soil should be humous and somewhat chalky, the situation warm and dry.

Cultivation: Propagate by soft cuttings from late spring until late summer. Plant out with a spacing of about 16 in (40 cm) on all sides. One plant is enough for a household unless you want it as an edging plant (e.g. for cottage-garden beds).

Give protection in severe winters. In spring cut back the shoots a little before they start into growth, to stop it straggling.

Harvest and preservation: Cut young shoot-tips from May to autumn. Harvest in summer so you can dry the non-woody shoots. Steeping in vinegar also preserves the flavour.

Active agents and application: Southernwood contains essential oils, tannins and bitter principles, which stimulate the

digestion and strengthen the stomach; very effective as a tea.

Add sparingly as a seasoning to salads, sauces and roasts, or as part of a stuffing for chicken.

Rue
(Ruta graveolens)

Botany: This southern European subshrub is a loner among herbs, belonging to the same family as the citrus fruits: Rutaceae. In June/July the delicate yellow flowers appear above the blue-green semi-evergreen foliage of rounded, filigree-like leaflets. The flowering plant is about 20–30 in (50–80 cm) tall.

Position: Chalky, free-draining soils, preferably low in nutrients, in a sunny situation.

rue starts to flower, and possibly again in late summer. Dry the shoots in the shade, then strip off the leaves.

Active agents and application: Essential oils, flavonoid glycosides, furocoumarins and alkaloids make rue a not entirely harmless plant. People with sensitive skins come out in a rash, and some of them can't bear even the smell. Even if you're not affected, you should avoid an excess of rue, particularly in pregnancy. Rue does have positive effects too: it's still used as an eyewash, and as a tea it has a calming action.

Rue can be used as a spice to add flavour to wine. It has a bitter taste, but stimulates the appetite when added in small quantities to sauces, substantial meat dishes, cheeses and salads.

Above *Southernwood is popular for low hedges in the cottage garden.*

Right *Rue is a pretty herb with attractive lacy foliage; the cultivar 'Jackman's Blue' has blue-grey leaves.*

Cultivation: Sow direct outside in April; plant out strong young plants at a spacing of 12 × 12 in (30 × 30 cm) — though one plant is ample for household use. You can also propagate by means of cuttings.

Cut the plant back a little before the winter, and in severe cold cover it with brushwood or something similar.

Harvest and preservation: You can take young leaves throughout most of the year. The main harvests are when the

A taste of summer

Cress
(Lepidium nanum)

Botany: Cress is an annual garden plant (the wild species come from the Near East) with both smooth- and curly-leaved varieties. It is one of the Cruciferae — the cabbage family. The flowers appear from May onwards, and it grows up to 20 in (50 cm) in height.

Position: Cress flourishes on fresh, humus-rich garden soils, and will even tolerate shady situations in summer.

Cress is a fast-growing herb that flourishes in the garden just as much as in shallow pans.

Cultivation: Sow the seeds (which need light) from March onwards, either broadcast or in rows 4 in (10 cm) apart; press in firmly and keep them moist until they germinate.

Cress grows well in mixed cultivation in the vegetable plot. But don't grow it again and again on the same patch, or it will deteriorate.

Cress can grow all year round in the greenhouse; in summer it's ready for harvest in as little as 10 days, but in winter it needs up to three weeks. For advice on growing cress on a window-sill, see page 22.

Harvest and preservation: The old leaves taste bitter; cut young shoots with a knife (or a scythe). If you grow cress in a seed-sprouter, you should harvest it just once, complete with the mat of roots.

Cress grows all year round, so there's no need apply any preservation methods.

Active agents and application: Cress contains bitter principles, mustard oils and lots of vitamin C, which combine to cleanse the blood and stimulate digestion.

The hottish flavour means that cress goes well with salads and low-fat vegetarian soft cheeses such as quark. It can also be used with many uncooked dishes, and makes a pleasant addition to sauces.

Dandelion
(Taraxacum officinale)

Botany: This well-known plant, with its 'dandelion clock' seeds and yellow composite flowers, is one of the most important and most undervalued native medicinal plants. The fleshy root is also used.

Position: Dandelions grow best in a sunny situation and fresh, rather heavy soils, rich in humus and nutrients; but they will grow anywhere.

Cultivation: Sow under glass in March/April and plant out in May, spacing 12 × 12 in (30 × 30

m) apart. Alternatively, sow
direct outside in rows from May
onwards.

After an August/September
sowing; don't harvest until the
following year. Otherwise grow
dandelion as an annual. In
summer, tie leaves together to
blanch them, or put them under
a flowerpot to keep them more
tender, and milder in flavour.

*Right With the cultivated dandelion
the leaves are blanched or the roots
forced into growth in the autumn,
like chicory.*

*Below You can pick young leaves
from meadow dandelions.*

If you want dandelion leaves
for your winter menu, dig up
the roots in October/November
(after a spring sowing) and cut
the leaves down to a finger's
breadth above them. Store
temporarily in a dark, cool but
frost-free place (in peat or sand
to stop them shrivelling).
Finally, set the roots in a bucket
with earth to force them into
growth, as with chicory. After
watering, keep them at 54–59°F
(12–15°C) and cover them to
exclude light, then harvest them
after 3–4 weeks. Special varieties are sold for this purpose.

Harvest and preservation: In
spring you can gather the young
leaves of meadow dandelions
growing in the wild, provided
they're not growing directly by
the road. Leaves are normally
used fresh, but can be dried as a
seasoning.

If you want to process the
roots, dig them up in autumn,
cut them open lengthways, and
hang them up somewhere airy
so that they can dry, too.

**Active agents and applica-
tion**: The great value of the
dandelion lies in its wide-
ranging mixture of active agents.
It contains bitter principles and
tannins, vitamins and minerals,
carbohydrates, organic acids,
essential oils and much more.
These constituents stimulate the
metabolism and cleanse the
blood, creating an urgent need
to pass water — the reason for
such popular local names as
'mess-a-bed', 'piss-a-bed' and
'wet-weed'.

You can make salads with the blanched leaves of dandelions, which are treated as a delicacy in France; they can also be added to soups and sauces, or even cooked like spinach.

You can use the leaves to make dandelion tea, but the main ingredient for this is the roots, crushed into small pieces and boiled. You can drink it to strengthen liver, stomach and gall-bladder; the well-known diuretic effect is valuable in the treatment of conditions such as gout and rheumatism. The ground-up roots can be roasted as a coffee substitute.

The fleshy leaves of summer purslane should only be used fresh.

Summer purslane
(Portulaca oleracea)

Botany: This annual plant from Asia is closely related to the sun plant (*P. grandiflora*); their generic name forms the basis for that of the botanical family — Portulacaceae.

The shoots of summer purslane bear succulent leaves and grow more than 12 in (30 cm) tall; yellowish flowers appear from June on. A creeping wild form can appear in sunny, sandy situations.

Position: To thrive, purslane needs a warm, sunny site and free-draining soil.

Cultivation: Once all danger of frost is past, sow the seed (which needs light to germinate) either broadcast or in rows 10 in (25 cm) apart. Keep them well moistened at first. As soon as the seedlings get crowded, thin them to 4 in (10 cm) apart within rows. Around the time of the first harvest, you can rake in some well-rotted garden compost between the rows. If the shoot-tips are removed, the plants develop a bushy habit.

Harvest and preservation: Take leaves and the tips of young shoots as soon as the plants are strong enough; older leaves have a bitter taste. Aim to harvest before the plant flowers. Three or four harvests a year are possible; the last one must be well before the first frost, since purslane is frost tender.

There's no sense in drying the fleshy shoots, but if necessary you can freeze or salt a surplus.

Active agents and application: Purslane is said to strengthen the stomach, cleanse the blood and act as a mild laxative, but its high vitamin content is its main asset.

The fresh shoots are good for salads and other uncooked dishes. They can also enrich the flavour of soups or be cooked like spinach. The flavour is bland, and the fleshy stems and leaves provide a lot of liquid.

Rocket
(Eruca vesicaria sativa)

Botany: This member of the Cruciferae comes from southern Europe and the Near East. It's known as an annual, but under favourable circumstances can be overwintered too. Rocket bears its yellowish or white flowers from May to October, reaching 20 in (50 cm) tall. It's easy to grow, it's available all season and it has an unusual taste.

Position: Humus-rich, fresh, but free-draining soil in a sunny to semi-shaded situation.

Cultivation: Sow successively direct into open ground from April/May on, about ½ in (1 cm) deep in rows 8 in (20 cm) apart. Thin out the seedlings a little later. If the position is too sunny, more flowers develop and the leaves taste more bitter. If you allow it to set seed, rocket will be self-seeding. It doesn't need much space and grows fast, so it's ideal for containers.

If you overwinter the plants in a sheltered spot, early leaves can

enrich an otherwise somewhat meagre menu as the cold weather draws to an end. To do this, it's best to start sowing from the middle of July on into September. You can grow rocket in the greenhouse at any time.

Harvest and preservation: Young, tender leaves up to 4 in (10 cm) high are chopped fresh and added to salads. Don't try to preserve rocket.

Active agents and application: Mustard oil and vitamins are what give rocket its flavour and its health-giving characteristics. Its delicious savoury flavour, best appreciated in the young leaves, makes it a piquant addition to salads in particular. You can also use it in sandwich fillings and in fresh seasoning mixtures.

Rocket thrives easily in situations that it likes, and its leaves have a unique savoury flavour.

Orache
(Atriplex hortensis)

Botany: This member of the Chenopodiaceae (goosefoot family) has become naturalised in Europe. It's an annual, long known both as a weed and as a cultivated plant.

Orache comes into flower from July onwards, by which time it has reached a height of at least 6 ft (1.8 m). As well as the common green garden form, there are yellow- and purple-leaved varieties.

Position: Undemanding; averagely fertilised, humus-rich garden soil and a little sun are all orache needs to flourish.

Orache is quick-growing, unde-manding and versatile.

Cultivation: Sow direct in open ground from March, in rows 18 in (45 cm) apart. Orache is a good, quick-growing plant for use in mixed cultivation. Keep the soil nice and moist (e.g. by using a mulch). If you keep picking the tips of the shoots, the plant develops a bushy habit. Orache self-seeds readily.

Harvest and preservation: Take shoot-tips and individual leaves continually, and a take full harvest shortly before flowering. Only use it fresh.

Active agents and application: Saponins without medicinal significance. With its mildly sour flavour, orache supplies vitamin C when eaten as a salad, prepared like spinach or used in soups and casseroles.

Salad burnet
(Sanguisorba minor)

Botany: Originally a native of southern Europe, this plant grows wild on dry meadows. Confusion is often caused by its close relationship to the great burnet *(S. officinalis)*, and by the name of the greater burnet saxifrage *(Pimpinella major)*, which is one of the Umbelliferae; the two burnets belong to the Rosaceae.

Salad burnet is an annual salad herb. In May/June small, roundish, green flower-heads, tinted red, appear on shoots from its rosettes of leaves; the flowers reach a height of 16 in (40 cm), and the whole plant may be as wide as it's tall.

Position: A warm situation on fresh, chalky, free-draining soil. On the whole, salad burnet is an undemanding plant.

Cultivation: Sow direct out of doors in April/May or September, in rows 14 in (35 cm) apart; thin later to 12 in (30 cm) within the rows. You can also divide existing plants.

Pinch out flower shoots promptly so that the plant puts its energies into developing leaves. In summer you may cut it back hard, which encourages stronger new growth. Remove any parts attacked by mildew. For the best plants, renew after two years.

Harvest and preservation: You can gather young leaves at any time. To preserve, you can either freeze the leaves, steep them in vinegar or oil, or else salt them.

If you want to use the roots, dig them up in October, wash them, and leave them to dry.

Active agents and application: Salad burnet is characterised by bitter principles, saponins and flavones, and also has plenty of vitamin C. It promotes digestion, staunches blood flow, and also acts as an antiseptic.

A tea is made from the root, or from leaves taken while the plant is in flower; it is used as a gargle.

The leaves taste similar to cucumber. As a flavouring they are only used raw, added to salads, sandwich fillings, soups and sauces, fish and eggs.

Reflexed stonecrop
(Sedum reflexum)

Botany: This succulent perennial has a creeping habit and bears little yellow flower heads from June until August. It grows wild all over Europe.

Position: Dry, stony or sandy low-lime soils in a sunny position (see page 13).

Cultivation: For ground cover, sow very shallow out of doors from April, thinning later to a spacing of 8 × 8 in (20 × 20 cm); once the seeds have germinated, there's no need to carry on watering. Otherwise, plant individual specimens in the rock garden; you can raise these as stem cuttings or buy them in from the garden centre. If it

likes its position, reflexed stonecrop will readily spread by itself.

Harvest and conservation: You can gather the fleshy leaves and tips of non-flowering shoots at any time. They aren't suitable for drying; it's best to freeze them or steep them in vinegar.

Active agents and application: With its bitter principles and mucilages, this herb has a slight blood-cleansing effect in salads and sauces, or when it's added to soups or to vegetable and meat dishes. It has no strong flavour of its own.

Salad burnet has just a slight taste of cucumber and contains lots of vitamin C.

Vitamins for colder weather

Scurvy grass
(Cochlearia officinalis)

Botany: This perennial member of the Cruciferae, grown here as a biennial, comes originally from Europe's seashores. From the May of its second year, the inflorescences appear above the spoon-shaped leaves at a height of 12-16 in (30–40 cm). Scurvy grass is sometimes known as spoonwort.

Position: This undemanding plant prefers fresh but friable soils containing salt. It also tolerates semi-shade.

Cultivation: Sow the seed (which need light to germinate) outside in March or April, in rows 8 in (20 cm) apart. For a winter harvest, sow in August or September, and before the plants start into growth again in spring, apply well-rotted garden

Similar cultivation, similar require-ments, and therefore so easy to confuse: **above** *winter purslane* (Claytonia perfoliata)*, also known as miner's lettuce or claytonia;* **left** *scurvy grass or spoonwort* (Cochlearia officinalis)*.*

compost or hoof-and-horn. Otherwise, apply fertiliser in the July after the first harvest. Keep the plants moist at all times.

If you grow scurvy grass in a garden frame or greenhouse, this will provide even more flexibility.

Harvest and preservation: The leaves can be cut all year round, even in snow — so there's no need to preserve

them. Take the main summer harvest before it flowers.

Active agents and application: Tannins, bitter principles and mustard oils determine the plant's medicinal effect and spicy flavour. But scurvy grass effectively owes its name to the high vitamin-C content, which makes it particularly valuable in winter. The squeezed juice promotes the digestion and is a pleasant spring tonic. Finely chopped fresh leaves can be added to salads, sandwich fillings, sauces or potato dishes. It can, however, irritate the mucous membranes, so don't eat large quantities.

Winter purslane
(Claytonia perfoliata)

Botany: A relative of summer purslane, this plant is sometimes known as miner's lettuce or claytonia, and came originally from North America. It grows as an annual cushion, and flowers in the first year after sowing. The leaves are heart-shaped, and fleshy when young.

Position: Likes fresh, humus-rich soil, and will also grow in semi-shaded situations.

Cultivation: The seed germinates only in temperatures below 54°F (12°C). Sow direct outside from April onwards,

Vitamins from the window-sill

To supply vitamins during the colder time of year, and for non-garden-owners, cress and many other species can be sown on the window-sill, either in dishes or as sprouting seeds.

First put the seeds in water until they swell, and then keep the temperature at 59-64°F (15-18°C) during germination. Once the seed-leaves have formed, try to give them as much light as possible: that way the vitamins are built up more readily, while harmful nitrates are more easily broken down. Rinse them through regularly to water them and remove any unwanted impurities.

Many other plants can be raised as sprouts in winter, notably some legumes (beans, peas, lentils), and also oats, barley, rye, linseed, radishes, fenugreek (*Trigonella foenum-graecum*), mustard, alfalfa and other new discoveries.

These vitamin sources are best consumed raw, mixed into salad, muesli or a soft cheese such as quark.

See also pictures and text on pages 24-25.

For watercress to develop its distinctive hottish taste, it must be kept constantly moist, maybe even in a pond or stream.

very shallow, either broadcast or in rows spaced 6-8 in (15-20 cm) apart; then harvest it until it flowers in the summer. If you sow in August/September, it's possible to harvest in winter. The growing time is shorter if you sow in a garden frame or greenhouse.

An application of well-rotted garden compost will encourage strong growth. To prevent the foliage cushion from freezing in winter, cover it with plastic sheet, brushwood or similar materials.

Harvest and preservation: Take fresh leaves at any time. If you grow it for the summer, you can take several harvests before it flowers. The little flowers look decorative, and can be eaten along with the leaves. When harvesting in winter, you can cut the shoots above ground two or three times. As it's available all year, no preservation is needed.

Active agents and application: Like most salad herbs, winter purslane stimulates the stomach and bowels. More important are the vitamin-C content and the sharp, fresh flavour, which makes it particularly suitable for salads and other uncooked dishes.

Watercress
(Nasturtium officinale)

Botany: This perennial member of the Cruciferae is found in streams and ponds all over Europe. White flowers appear from May onwards, and flowering stems can reach 24 in (60 cm) in height.

Position: In or on the edge of a garden pond or stream, or in a bog garden or earth-filled stone sink — must *always* be wet.

Cultivation: It's best to sow from June onwards in a growing medium that is kept wet at all times, with 1-2 in (2-5 cm) of water standing above the surface. In August or September, plant it out in its final position so that the shoot-tips just peep out above the surface of the water. In subsequent years this is the time to take cuttings 4-6 in (10-15 cm) long and root them in water.

If watercress is growing on its own, you may apply a liquid feed to the soil and water after the harvest; but this isn't a good idea in a garden pond.

Harvest and preservation: Starting as early as the October of the first year, cut young shoots and leaves, repeating this every 5 weeks or so. Store it in cold water until you need it.

You can harvest watercress all winter in areas with a favourable climate (or from containers in a sheltered position), so there is usually no need to preserve it; if you do, then you should dry it in the shade.

Active agents and application: Vitamins, minerals (especially iron) and mustard oil (which determines the taste) stimulate the metabolism and help cleanse the blood.

The cress-like, slightly hot taste goes well in salads and other uncooked dishes, but don't indulge to excess over a long period, especially if you're pregnant.

Yellow rocket
(Barbarea vulgaris)

Botany: Also called winter cress, this herb is yet another member of the Cruciferae, and comes from southern Europe. The yellow flowers first appear above the foliage rosette in the April of its second year, and it grows up to 30 in (80 cm).

Position: Yellow rocket grows happily in the semi-shade on fresh, loamy soils rich in humus and nutrients.

Cultivation: From April onwards, sow direct outside in rows 8 in (20 cm) apart — or sow in August/September for subsequent harvesting up until 4 December (St Barbara's Day). Thin out later to 8 in (20 cm) within rows. A layer of mulch will help to keep the moisture in the soil. Yellow rocket can even be harvested through the winter if it's under a protective cover.

*Yellow rocket (*Barbarea vulgaris*) can be harvested up to St Barbara's Day, 4 December.*

Harvest and preservation: Grown for the summer, the feathery leaves and shoot-tips can be picked fresh from May to July, but don't take the leaves that grow on the flower stalks. In cold weather, pick the leaves for as long as they are accessible. Only use them fresh.

Active agents and application: Yellow rocket has no medicinal significance. The mustard oil gives it a flavour similar to that of cress. The vitamin-C content is best maintained if it's eaten raw, as in salads — but you can also cook it like spinach.

Flowering salads

Borage
(Borago officinalis)

Botany: This annual herb has given its name to the family Boraginaceae. It self-seeds so readily that it's easy to forget its Mediterranean and Oriental origins. The vivid-blue flowers, a favourite 'pasture' for bees, appear from June to November, growing to 40 in (1 m) or more.

Position: Prefers a sunny situation and soils rich in humus and nutrients, fresh but free-draining, and somewhat chalky.

Cultivation: Sow direct outside from April to June in rows 10 in (25 cm) apart; ideally, grow it mixed in the vegetable plot. Borage needs little attention other than occasional hoeing, and watering in dry weather.

Harvest and preservation: Take young leaves and flowers to use fresh at any time from June onwards. The soft leaves are frost-tender and difficult to preserve: steeping in vinegar still works best.

Active agents and application: Thanks to the presence of saponins, along with mucilages and tannins, borage cleanses the blood and strengthens the heart.

The raw leaves, which taste like cucumber, are ideal for salads, quark dishes, eggs, potatoes and fish. The little blue starry flowers are also edible, making an attractive garnish on the plate, or for wine cups and fruit drinks in summer.

Marigold
(Calendula officinalis)

Botany: This annual member of the Compositae comes from southern Europe and Asia. With its glowing yellow and orange flowers, marigold has won a place in the ornamental garden. Height up to 2 ft (60 cm).

Position: Mostly undemanding, preferring free-draining chalky soils in sunny situations.

Cultivation: Sow direct outside from April onwards, in rows 10 in (25 cm) apart. Marigolds are ideal for mixed cultivation in the vegetable plot; they spread spontaneously by themselves.

Harvest and preservation: Cut and dry the flowers soon after they've opened. Add young leaves to salad, and use

Borage leaves taste like cucumber, and the flowers provide an edible garnish.

the yellow flower petals as a seasoning (or as a substitute for saffron).

Active agents and application: Essential oils, saponins and vitamin-like substances make the marigold a valuable medicinal plant. In cases of wounds or sprains, you can make compresses with a tea.

Nasturtium
(Tropaeolum majus)

Botany: This annual border and balcony plant comes originally from Peru. The hanging or climbing varieties grow no higher than 12 in (30 cm) when planted as ground cover, though when climbing they can reach

5–6 ft (1.5–1.8 m); these start flowering as early as June.

Position: Nasturtiums are relatively undemanding. They need soil with good supplies of humus; it should be on the heavy side but also free-draining. The plants are highly toleraant of semi-shade.

Cultivation: Sow under glass in April, or direct outside from May onwards, the final spacing should be 8 × 4 in (20 × 10 cm). Applying nitrogen-rich fertiliser produces more leaves, not more flowers.

Harvest and preservation: Pick fresh leaves and flowers continually. They aren't suitable

Left *Not only beautiful, but also a valuable medicinal plant: the marigold*

Right *The flowers of the nasturtium are just as tasty as the leaves.*

for preserving, but the flower buds can be pickled in vinegar as a substitute for capers.

Active agents and application: Nasturtiums contain mustard oils and plenty of vitamins; these cleanse the blood, promote digestion and improve the body's general resistance.

With their sharp, spicy flavour, the young shoots are good in salads and sandwiches. The flowers are equally tasty, and make an unusual decoration.

Wild herbs for salads

The herbs in this section are described chiefly in terms of their application. If you can't identify them positively yourself, buy a good plant guide or take a knowledgeable friend before you go out collecting them in the wild. And always remember that any rare plants should *never* be collected in the wild.

Stinging nettle
(Urtica dioica, U. urens)

Botany: Nettles have lent their generic name to a whole botanical family — the Urticaceae — and are indigenous throughout the world. The larger stinging nettle *(U. dioica)*, up to 5 ft (1.5 m) tall, spreads principally by means of yellow subterranean runners. The smaller nettle *(U. urens)*, around 20 in (50 cm) tall, sows itself afresh each year. Clusters of greenish-white flowers appear from July onwards. Nettles are food plants for many butterfly species.

Position: The larger nettle prefers nutrient-rich rubbish dumps or woodland edges; the small nettle prefers open fields.

Harvest and preservation: The young shoots can be picked almost all year, the flowers from July, and the stalks and roots in autumn. The leaves are most nutritious when fresh, but can also be dried.

Active agents and application: As well as formic acid (the stinging agent) and other fatty acids, nettles contain vitamins and minerals. They improve blood development, metabolism and bile secretion, and are useful in cases of gout or rheumatism (as a diuretic tea or as a bath). You can obtain a tough bast (flexible plant fibre) from the stalks.

Young shoots can be cooked like spinach, added to spring salads or made into soup. The inflorescences sweated in butter are regarded as a delicacy.

Sorrel
(Rumex species)

Botany: This perennial member of the Polygonaceae (knotweed family) reaches 30 in (80 cm) with its inflorescences, which appear from May to July.

To grow English sorrel (*R. acetosa*), use one of its cultivars: their leaves are more tender, and milder in flavour.

Among the other edible wild sorrels are sheep sorrel (*R. acetosella*) and curly dock (*R. crispus*). Another good species is French or shield sorrel (*R.*

You should only let the stinging nettles proliferate where they won't bother anyone.

The cultivated form of sorrel forms strong, leafy shoots with a sour-sharp flavour.

scutatus), with its somewhat rounded, fleshy, grey-green leaves. The latter self-seeds readily.

Position: Sorrel likes moist, nutrient-rich meadows on acid, humus-rich, heavyish soils. When cultivated, it will tolerate semi-shade.

Growing sorrel cultivars: Sow the seed very shallow outside from March to May in rows 12 in (30 cm) apart, thinning later to 12 in (30 cm) within rows. You can also propagate by division. Give the young crop an application of manure or nitrogen-rich fertiliser, especially if you want to take several harvests. Remove inflorescences, and keep the soil moist. Self-seeding occurs freely.

Harvest and preservation: From April right into November, you can cut young leaves at any time, but leave the heart alone! Avoid older leaves because they contain high concentrations of poisonous oxalic acid. You can freeze chopped leaves in ice.

Active agents and application: Sorrel contains vitamin C, oxalic acid and minerals that cleanse the blood and stimulate the appetite. The sharp, fresh flavour goes well with salads and sandwich fillings, and (cooked very briefly) with soups, sauces and meat dishes. French sorrel makes a delicious soup on its own. Use sparingly, as some people react badly to it.

Daisy
(Bellis perennis)

Botany: One of our commonest native flowers, the daisy belongs to the Compositae, and flowers from April to October.

Position: Likes plenty of humus and nutrients, grows readily in lawns and verges, and likes a sunny situation. The double daisy variety is cultivated as a biennial spring flower.

Harvest and preservation: Take young leaves and flowers almost all year round (though they are best in the spring). Daisies can also be dried.

Active agents and application: A daisy tea is good for catarrhal coughs because of the saponins it contains. Spring salads with daisies are also marvellous for stimulating the metabolism.

75

Ground elder, goutweed
(Aegopodium podagraria)

Botany: A native wild umbellifer regarded by gardeners as a troublesome weed, and spreading by means of a creeping rootstock. White inflorescences appear from June to August, growing up to 30 in (80 cm).

Position: Forms woodland undergrowth; grows on fresh, humus-rich soils; acceptable if it can't spread to other beds.

Harvest and preservation: Pick fresh shoots at any time, but most of all in spring. For larger quantities, harvest it before flowering and dry it.

Active agents and application: The essential oils of goutweed were once used as compresses or poultices for gout — hence the name. Young leaves can be used in salads or soups, or cooked like spinach.

If the ground elder is clogging up the garden, just eat it!

Ramsons is best harvested before it flowers. The aroma makes it quite unmistakable.

Ramsons
(Allium ursinum)

Botany: This perennial relative of the onion grows about 12 in (30 cm) high and bears white flowers as early as April, giving off a strong scent of garlic.

Position: Mostly in the shade of moist, nutrient-rich deciduous woodland. In the garden, grow it next to woody plants.

Harvest and preservation: Take young leaves, best just before flowering. The distinctive smell should make confusion with other plants impossible. There's no reason to preserve it.

Active agents and preservation: With its sulphurous essential oils, vitamins and minerals, ramsons in many ways resembles its close relative, garlic. It cleanses the blood, strengthens and disinfects, especially when chopped up raw in spring salads or sandwich fillings. Soups and vegetable dishes can also be enriched with ramsons.

Milfoil, yarrow
(Achillea millefolium)

Botany: This well-known herbaceous perennial belongs to the family Compositae, and is found throughout most of the Northern Hemisphere. From June into October, the false umbels coloured white to pink rise to over 20 in (50 cm) above finely feathered leaves.

Position: Milfoil is undemanding, but likes dry meadows and

Above *A versatile medicinal plant, suitable for salads too — the milfoil or yarrow*

Below *Ribwort plantain leaves can cure both coughs and wounds.*

path edges. To cultivate it, you can divide clumps of it or take cuttings in spring.

Harvest and preservation: Take young leaves for salad in spring. From June to September, cut soft shoot sections — in flower, if at all possible — for making a tea. Dry in the shade to preserve it.

Active agents and application: The numerous active agents contained in milfoil were once used to regulate menstruation and staunch blood from wounds. The tea can still be used to relieve inflammation and spasms, helping to treat various illnesses. Employ it cautiously, as not everyone can tolerate it.

In salads, herb soft cheese or soups, the young leaves make an enriching spring tonic.

Ribwort plantain
(Plantago lanceolata)

Botany: Ribwort plantain blooms from May onwards; the flower spikes with their delicate white stamens grow some 12 in (30 cm) above the rosettes of leaves. Its various broad-leaved relatives in the Plantaginaceae (plantain family) also have medicinal properties.

Position: Dry, fresh meadows and path edges.

Harvest and preservation: Take young leaves in spring as a wild vegetable, and all year round for the tea. Before making the tea, you must first chop the leaves up and dry them in the shade.

Active agents and application: A valuable cough remedy if taken as a tea sweetened with honey or as a juice. Crushed leaves are used to heal wounds. Mix fresh leaves into salads for a spring tonic.

Salad herbs by seasons

Harvest calendar — mainly cultivated species (arranged by time of harvest)

Name	Harvest time	Parts of plant	Sowing	Natural habitat	Ann/ peren	Plant family	Taste
garden cress (*Lepidium nanum*)	all year	young shoots	from 3 (all year)	(also shaded)	ann	Cruciferae	hot
dandelion (*Taraxacum officinale*)	3–7 (winter)	young/ blanched leaves	5 (gl 3–4)	nutrient-rich meadows	peren	Compositae	mildly spicy
garden sorrel (*Rumex acetosa*)	4–9	young leaves	3–5	nutrient-rich meadows	peren	Polygonaceae	slightly sharp
comfrey (*Symphytum officinale*)	4–9	young leaves	3–4	damp meadows	peren	Boraginaceae	fresh
orache (*Atriplex hortensis*)	5–9	shoot tips and leaves	3	weed	ann	Chenopodiaceae	mildly sharp
summer purslane (*Portulaca oleracea*)	5–10	young shoots and leaves	5–6	weed on warm, sandy sites	ann	Portulacaceae	mildly spicy, sharp
reflexed stonecrop (*Sedum reflexum*)	5–10	shoot tips and leaves	4–5	stony soil or rock garden	peren	Crassulaceae	spicy
rocket (*Eruca vesicaria sativa*)	5–11	young leaves	4–5	free-draining, self-seeding	ann	Cruciferae	hot, savoury
borage (*Borago officinalis*)	6–10	young leaves and flowers	4–6	goes wild in the garden	ann	Boraginaceae	cucumber-like
salad burnet (*Sanguisorba minor*)	6–10	young leaves	4–5	dry meadows	peren	Rosaceae	cucumber-like
nasturtium (*Tropaeolum majus*)	6–11	leaves and flowers	5 (gl 4)	around bases of trees	ann	Tropaeolaceae	cress-like
scurvy grass (*Cochlearia officinalis*)	6–3	leaves	8–9	coast	bien	Cruciferae	mildly spicy
watercress (*Nasturtium officinale*)	10–3 (all year)	young shoots and leaves	6	edge of stream or pond	peren	Cruciferae	cress-like
yellow rocket (*Barbarea vulgaris*)	11–3	shoot tips and leaves	8–9	damp hedgerows	ann	Cruciferae	cress-like
winter purslane (*Claytonia perfoliata*)	11–4 (6–7)	leaves	8–9	(semi-shaded)	ann	Portulacaceae	sharp, fresh

Salad herbs — mainly species growing in the wild (arranged by time of collection)

Name	Harvest time	Parts of plant	Natural habitat	Ann/peren	Plant family	Taste
common daisy (*Bellis perennis*)	all year	young	flower meadows	peren	Compositae	mildly spicy
shepherd's purse (*Capsella bursa-pastoris*)	3–4	young leaves	meadows, paths and rubbish tips	ann	Cruciferae	spicy
ramsons (*Allium ursinum*)	3–5	young leaves	woodlands and hedgerows	peren	Liliaceae	garlic-like
milfoil, yarrow (*Achillea millefolium*)	3–5	young leaves	dry meadows	peren	Compositae	spicy
greater burnet saxifrage (*Pimpinella major* 'Rosea')	3–6	young leaves	dry meadows	peren	Umbelliferae	spicy
ground ivy, goutweed (*Glechoma hederacea*)	3–6	young shoots	meadows and paths	peren	Labiatae	spicy, bitterish
brooklime (*Veronica beccabunga*)	3–9	shoot tips and leaves	banks of ponds or streams	peren	Scrophulariaceae	mildly spicy
chicory, wild succory (*Cichorium intybus*)	4–5	young leaves	path edges	peren	Compositae	fresh, bitterish
Good King Henry (*Chenopodium bonushenricus*)	4–5	young leaves	pastures and rubbish tips	ann	Chenopodiaceae	sharp
garlic mustard (*Alliaria officinalis*)	4–5	young leaves	path edges and hedgerows	bien	Cruciferae	garlic-like
ground elder, goutweed (*Aegopodium podagraria*)	4–6	young leaves	woodland undergrowth (root-spreading weed)	peren	Umbelliferae	sharp, spicy
ribwort plantain (*Plantago lanceolata*)	4–6	young leaves	meadows and paths	peren	Plantaginaceae	faintly salty, mild
stinging nettle (*Urtica dioica, U. urens*)	4–6 (4–11)	young shoots and leaves	nutrient-rich weedy corner	peren	Urticaceae	aromatic
white deadnettle (*Lamium album*)	4–8	young shoots and leaves	path edges	peren	Labiatae	tasty
sorrel (*Rumex acetosa*)	4–11	young leaves	nutrient-rich meadows	peren	Polygonaceae	sharp and fresh
common agrimony (*Agrimonia eupatoria*)	6–9	flowering shoot tips	hedgerows, infertile meadows	peren	Rosaceae	spicy

Key: 1–12 = months of the year/January–December; gl = sown under glass; ann = annual; bien = biennial; peren = perennial

Medicinal herbs in cultivation

Wild camomile
(Matricaria recutita)

Botany: An annual field weed of the family Compositae, originally from south-eastern Europe. From May to October it displays little yellow flower heads and white, folded-back petals. Some cultivars contain particularly large amounts of active agents.

Position: Prefers loamy but free-draining field soils, or rubbish dumps in a sunny situation.

Cultivation: Sow direct out of doors in April or September, either broadcast or in rows 12 in (30 cm) apart; thin later if necessary. Keep soil loose by hoeing.

Harvest and preservation: Take flower-heads when the white petals turn down, ideally in sunny weather. Then spread them out to dry gently in an airy location.

Active agents and application: Essential oils, flavonoids and coumarins help inflammations and wounds. The tea calms stomach cramps. A compress heals external complaints, and inhaling the vapour relieves throat inflammation. An infusion of the flower heads makes a soothing and calming drink.

A distinguishing feature of the wild camomile: the reflexed white petals

Valerian
(Valeriana officinalis)

Botany: Valerian grows to around 5 ft (1.5 m) in height, and bears white-to-pink-toned inflorescences from May to August (see picture, page 29).

Position: Valerian grows on humus-rich stream banks, in damp meadows, around the edges of woodlands, in gardens and on dry, sandy sites; it likes semi-shade.

Cultivation: You can sow the seeds from April onwards, but without covering them. It's better to buy the plants and place them in a herb bed or at the edge of woodland.

Valerian likes an application of rotted garden compost. Pull out the flower shoots before harvesting the roots.

Harvest and preservation: In September or October, dig out the roots of strong plants; then clean, chop and dry them ready for use. You can dry them in an oven on a low heat.

Active agents and application: The essential oils and alkaloids produce a calming effect. A tea made from the roots helps with insomnia, nervous stress and similar conditions.

Elecampane
(Inula helenium)

Botany: This herbaceous perennial from the Near East is now naturalised in our woods and cottage gardens. Yellow composite flowers with thin, thread-like petal appear from June to September. The flowering stems can be more than 6 ft 6 in (2 m) tall.

Position: Grow elecampane in deep, fresh, humus-rich soils in sun to semi-shade.

Cultivation: Elecampane is best sown under glass from mid-March onwards; plant out from May onwards, spaced at 20×20 in (50×50 cm).

This plant grows well in between herbaceous perennials against a fence. It will take generous applications of rotted garden compost and organic fertilisers.

Left *The roots of the elecampane are used to make a tea for coughs.*

Right *With the common mallow, the leaves contain the active agents.*

Harvest and preservation: Dig out the roots in October/November, and possibly also in spring. After cleaning them, halve them lengthways. Dry them in a well-ventilated place, and finally store them in an airtight container.

Active agents and application: Essential oils, inulin, and bitter principles improve the metabolism and soothe a tickly throat. This plant was once used as a cure for absolutely everything. Nowadays a tea made from dried, ground-up roots is used for coughs.

Common mallow
(Malva sylvestris)

Botany: Local names for this plant include bread-and-cheese and pancake plant. The common mallow usually flowers from the May of its second year, producing beautiful violet to pink blooms and growing to 40 in (1 m) or more.

Various other native members of the mallow family are also known to have similar healing properties.

Position: Mallow grows on the humus-rich, free-draining edges of paths and fields; in the garden it likes sunny spots against walls and fences.

Cultivation: Soak the seed first, then (because it has tap roots)

it's best to sow it broadcast out of doors between April and June without transplanting it later. Thin it later to about 12 × 16 in (30 × 40 cm). It also grows well in open herbaceous borders or vegetable plots.

Harvest and preservation: Take young leaves in the spring; gather flowers, with their stems, from June onwards, and dry them in a shaded but airy place.

Active agents and application: Mucilages and tannins enable mallow tea to alleviate coughs, colds and sore throats; allow it to draw for several hours, then gargle with it. Mallow can also be used externally for skin rashes. Its leaves can be prepared and eaten as a vegetable.

81

This bergamot variety is unsuitable for making a tea — use only the scarlet-flowered species.

Marsh mallow
(Althaea officinalis)

Botany: A perennial member of the mallow family (Malvaceae) that comes from the eastern Mediterranean. It grows taller than the common mallow, bearing pale lilac-pink flowers from June until August. Its leaves are soft and velvety.

Position: Open, fresh, moist, humus-rich soil in a warm situation; sun to semi-shade.

Cultivation: Sow in seed-bed from April onwards, and transplant from June or in autumn, spaced 16 × 16 in (40 × 40 cm). You can also detach suckers in spring. Keep the ground moist.

Harvest and preservation: Take flowering herb in summer; gentle drying possible. Roots are the main crop: dig them out in November (starting the second year); wash, chop and dry (e.g. in oven on a very low heat).

Active agents and application: The tea is used as a gargle (put roots to draw in cold water); mucilages relieve irritation in upper respiratory tract.

Red bergamot
(Monarda didyma)

Botany: A North American perennial belonging to the mint family and established as an ornamental; for medicinal purposes use only the scarlet forms. Known as Oswego tea, Indian's plume or bee balm, it grows to over 40 in (1 m); flowers (June to October) attractive to bees.

Position: Fresh garden soils, rich in humus and nutrients, in a predominantly sunny situation.

Cultivation: Uncultivated form hard to find. Take root-tip cuttings, or divide in spring, spacing at 16 × 16 in (40 × 40 cm). Supply regularly with well-rotted garden compost. After 3 years divide clumps and replant.

Harvest and preservation: Take fresh leaves at any time; main harvest during flowering season; dry in an airy place.

Active agents and application: The anthocyanins, tannins and bitter principles make a refreshing digestive tea.

Angelica
(Angelica archangelica)

Botany: A short-lived perennial belonging to the Umbelliferae and found throughout Europe. Imposing inflorescences (from July of the second year) grow up to 8 ft (2.5 m) tall.

Position Needs deep, nutrient-rich soils, moist but free-draining, in a sunny to semi-shaded situation.

Cultivation: Sow in September or October in open ground or a garden frame; transplant to final position the following spring. One plant is normally enough, but if not, space 32–40 in (80–100 cm) apart. Cover only with garden compost that has rotted completely.

Harvest and preservation: From July, take young leaves and shoots as a seasoning. Dig roots up in the autumn, starting the second year; cut them open lengthways and dry, then grind small and store in a container.

Left *Heavenly help for the digestion — angelica*

Right *St Mary's thistle strengthens the liver and can soothe the eyes.*

Active agents and application: A tea made from the roots contains essential oils, organic acids and bitter principles that calm the digestion and stimulate the appetite.

The leaves and young shoots can be used for seasoning and as a vegetable. Peel and cook the stems in sugar syrup to make a compote, or use candied stems for cake decoration.

St Mary's thistle, milk thistle
(Silybum marianum)

Botany: This Mediterranean member of the Compositae is an annual thistle growing to 5 ft (1.5 m). It has marbled prickly leaves, and flowers from June to August; survives a mild winter.

Position: Free-draining, rather infertile garden soil in a sun-drenched situation.

Cultivation: Sow from March onwards in a garden frame, or from mid-April in the seed-bed. Plant out after mid-May, when there is no risk of frost, spaced at 12 × 16 in (30 × 40 cm). Good for mixed cultivation in the vegetable plot.

Harvest and preservation: Before the seeds fall out, but when they're as ripe as possible, separate them from the white down. Let them dry thoroughly.

Active agents and application: Bitter principles and essential oils, mainly in the seed-case. A tea made from the seeds helps to strengthen a weak liver.

Medicinal herbs from the wild

Milfoil, yarrow
(Achillea millefolium)
See page 76.

Ribwort plantain
(Plantago lanceolata)
See page 77.

Comfrey
(Symphytum officinale)

Botany: This perennial relative of borage is a native of this country, growing to 5 ft (1.5 m). Its flower clusters (May–August) are a good food source for insects. Blue comfrey *(S. peregrinum)* contains even more valuable ingredients.

Position: In full sun on deep, moist, nutrient-rich soils; also semi-shaded.

Cultivation: In April, plant rootstocks 2 in (5 cm) deep, spaced at 20 × 20 in (50 × 50 cm). When they've taken root, apply some well-rotted garden compost or other organic fertiliser to make sure they develop

Above *Although controversial — it is, after all, a pernicious weed — the coltsfoot is irreplaceable in naturopathy.*

Left *Comfrey is good for healing wounds.*

strongly. A layer of mulch helps to keep the ground moist.

Harvest and preservation: Harvest the young leaves at any time during the growing season. The roots of older plants are best dug up and washed in April/May or October/November. They'll dry most quickly if split lengthways; after drying, store in an airtight container.

Active agents and application: With its valuable proteins, vitamins, alkaloids, tannins and mucilages, comfrey is an extremely versatile medicinal herb. The leaves are very tasty if you brown them quickly in hot fat or cook them like spinach.

The leaves are used for mulching, animal feed and liquid fertilisers (see page 95), and medicinally in compresses for use with sprains, wounds or even rheumatism (though for this a paste made from the roots is more effective). Other preparations include ointments on a lanolin-oil base, and tinctures in brandy.

Coltsfoot
(Tussilago farfara)

Botany: A native herbaceous perennial, and one of the earliest-flowering plants in the year, producing yellow composite flowers 8–10 in (20–25 cm) high from February to April. The leaves, reminiscent of butterbur, appear only after flowering.

Position: Soils with plenty of lime, clay and loam, and also scree; preferably in the sun. Often grows along the edges of paths, hedges and rubbish tips.

Cultivation: Either bring plants into the garden after flowering, or sow under glass in February, planting out later. But always remember that coltsfoot is extremely invasive and hard to eradicate, spreading rapidly by means of runners — so it's best kept strictly confined, even when growing in a wild garden.

Harvest and preservation: Pick the flowers in February or March. Then collect the leaves from May to July; chop them up and finally and dry them.

Active agents and application: Thanks to the mucilages and bitter principles contained in coltsfoot, it has become a well-tried cough remedy. Coltsfoot tea reduces soreness and irritation, and relieves congestion in colds and flu. But you should never take it in large doses or over an extended period, particularly during pregnancy.

The young leaves can be cooked like a vegetable.

Mullein
(Verbascum densiflorum)

Botany: This plant is a member of the foxglove family (Scrophulariaceae). In the second year after sowing, the flower stems grow up to 8 ft (2.5 m) tall above the rosettes of down-covered leaves, and hosts of small flower calyxes open one after another throughout the summer. After this, despite the strong tap root, the mullein must seed itself afresh.

Position: Chalky, rather free-draining soils in sunny situations sheltered from the wind.

Cultivation: Sow in the seed-bed or *in situ* in June/July, transplanting if necessary in the autumn.

The flowers of the mullein must be picked off regularly.

Harvest and preservation: The fully formed flowers are very delicate, so you should only gather them in the morning when they are dry. To preserve them, dry them in the shade, and store them in a dark container.

Active agents and application: Mullein contains various mucilages that are highly beneficial in the treatment of coughs, colds and the like. The tea has proved especially invaluable for dealing with dry coughs. When used as an oil, mullein has proved an excellent remedy for neuralgia.

The cheerful little faces of the wild pansy look as if they were specially made to relieve children's illnesses.

Wild pansy, heartsease
(Viola tricolor)

Botany: The wild or field pansy develops colourful flowers (far smaller than those of the garden varieties) from May onwards during its second and final year of life. This relative of the violet can grow to a height of about 12 in (30 cm).

Position: Grows like a weed on free-draining, humus-rich soils in fields, meadows and rubbish tips, in sun to semi-shade.

Cultivation: Sow from April onwards; plant in autumn.

Harvest and preservation: Cut and dry the flowering herb from May to September. After drying it, crumble it up small and store it in a sealed contain-er. The roots are even richer in active agents.

Active agents and application: Saponins and a flavone glycoside have a diuretic and blood-cleansing action. Wild pansy is used as a tea ingredient for some childhood ailments, and also for gout.

Great burdock
(Arctium lappa)

Botany: This biennial member of the Compositae grows up to 5 ft (1.5 m) tall from July onwards, when the spherical flowers with their 'sticky' barbs appear.

Position: Free-draining, humus-rich soils on a sunny site. Grows well at the edge of a path or hedge, on fields or rubbish tips.

Right *Great burdock may be a nuisance when it gets caught in woollens, but it's a valuable medicinal plant.*

Below *An attractive tree for broad avenues and country estates, the small-leaved lime is indispensable as a medicinal plant.*

Cultivation: Sow direct outside in June/July.

Harvest and preservation: Harvest the roots from the October of the second year. Clean and chop them, then dry them (e.g. in the oven on a low heat).

Active agents and application: Essential oils, tannins, mucilages and large amounts of inulin mean that great burdock can be used for a wide variety of applications. It can be used to make compresses for wounds and ulcers, and even for a hair tonic. The tea stimulates bile production and cleanses the blood. Young shoots can be eaten as a vegetable.

Small-leaved lime
(Tilia cordata)

Botany: This well-known tree grows to over 100 ft (30 m). The scented, yellowy flower clusters start appearing in June. The small-leaved lime is commoner than its relative the large-leaved lime *(T. platyphyllos)*.

Position: Likes deep, humus-rich soils; native to mixed woodlands in mild situations.

Cultivation: Plant in spring or autumn. This tree grows too large for most modern gardens.

Harvest and preservation: Harvest the flowers individually several times, complete with the bracts, and as soon as possible after they open. Then dry them thoroughly and store in a dark, airtight container.

Active agents and application: Lime contains valuable essential oils and mucilages. The tea is good for treating colds, not only as a decongestant, but even more especially for inducing a sweat.

Left *Bramble leaves are often put in tea mixtures.*

Right *The cultivated form of lady's mantle has no medicinal properties.*

Blackberry, bramble
(Rubus fruticosus)

Botany: Prickly thorn-bearing shrub, up to 6 ft (2 m) high and inclined to run wild. It produces white or pale-purple flowers from June until August, but the fruits go on into October.

Position: Humus-rich, free-draining damp soils in sunny to semi-shaded situations. Occurs naturally in clearings and hedgerows. Also grows on bare gravelly areas.

Cultivation: In spring or autumn, plant young bushes or rooted pieces of shoots (obtained by tip layering).

Harvest and preservation: For medicinal purposes, harvest young leaves in the spring; chop them and dry them.

Active agents and application: Tannins and vitamin C make bramble leaves a valuable constituent of home tea blends, for fever and stomach ailments.

Lady's mantle
(Alchemilla xanthochlora syn. *A. vulgaris* hort.)

Botany: This perennial is a member of the rose family. The yellowy-green flower tufts appear in May above the attractive foliage. Lady's mantle in the wild is seldom taller than 12 in (30 cm), but some of the garden varieties can grow as high as 20 in (50 cm).

Position: Lady's mantle likes moist, humus-rich soil in sun to semi-shade. In the wild it grows on nutrient-rich mountain meadows, and also near the banks of streams.

Cultivation: Raise under glass in February/March. The garden form is valued as ground cover in shady herbaceous borders or next to a garden pond, but it has no medicinal value.

Harvest and preservation: Harvest the leaves and flowers from May through the summer, chop and dry them in the shade.

Active agents and application: As its name suggests, lady's mantle possesses tannins and related substances that provide remedies specifically for women. The tea is mostly used to alleviate menstruation problems and in preparation for childbirth. It also helps to heal various types of inflammation.

St John's wort
(Hypericum perforatum)

Botany: This species is more precisely called perforated St John's wort because of the translucent spots on the leaves. A herbaceous perennial growing up to 40 in (1 m) tall. From June to September it displays shiny-yellow flowers with delicate filaments reminiscent of rays of sunshine. Related species are used as ground cover.

Position: Likes free-draining soils in warm, sunny situations, often next to paths or clumps of bushes; sometimes also found on rubbish tips.

Cultivation: Sow under glass from February/March, or direct outside in a well-prepared seed-bed from April onwards; plant out in spring or autumn.

Harvest and preservation: Cut the flowering herb off, about 6–9 in (15–23 cm) above the ground, on or around the 24 June (the Feast of the Nativity of St John the Baptist); dry it in the shade. St John's wort is most effective when preserved in olive oil.

Active agents and application: The principal active agents are an essential oil, a tannin and various resins. The oil is suitable for external application to heal wounds and treat rheumatic complaints. The tea has a calming effect, and is even used to combat depression. But you should never use it over long periods, as St John's wort causes great sensitivity to sunshine.

To obtain an oil extract of St John's wort, take about 1 oz of the dried herb, rub it finely and mix it into 1 pt olive oil (about 25 g into 500 ml). Leave the mixture to ferment for three to five days in an open, translucent bottle. Then close the bottle up tightly, and stand it in the sun for about six weeks. By now the contents should have taken on a red colour. Strain the oil, firmly squeezing out the residue, and transfer it to a dark, airtight bottle for storage.

St John's wort possesses remarkable healing properties, but it should never be used to excess.

Herbs for the home medicine cabinet

Name	Harvest time	Parts of plant	Natural habitat	Ann/ peren	Cultiva- tion	Prepara- tion
Respiratory tract (coughs etc.)						
common mallow (*Malva sylvestris*)	4-7	young leaves and flowers	sunny edges of paths	bien	sd 6	tea
ribwort plantain (*Plantago lanceolata*)	4-10	leaves	paths and meadows	peren	–	tea
coltsfoot (*Tussilago farfara*)	5-7 (2-3)	young leaves (flowers)	path edges, rubbish tips	peren	sd 2, pl 5	tea
thyme (*Thymus vulgaris*)	5-8	young shoots	dry, warm	peren	pl 5	tea
sage (*Salvia officinalis*)	5-9	leaves	free-draining, warm	peren	pl 4-5	tea
mullein (*Verbascum densiflorum*)	7-8	flowers	sunny and free-draining	bien	sd 6-7	tea
anise (*Pimpinella anisum*)	8-9	seed	sunny garden	bien	sd 4	tea
elecampane (*Inula helenium*)	10-11	roots	path edges	peren	gl 3-4, pl 5	tea
marsh mallow (*Althaea officinalis*)	11 (6-8)	roots (flowering herb)		peren	gl 4, pl 6	tea
Colds						
blackberry, bramble (*Rubus fruticosus*)	4-5	leaves and flowers	hedgerows	shrub	pl 4 or 10	tea
small-leaved lime (*Tilia cordata*)	6-7	flowers	woods and avenues	tree	pl 4 or 10	tea
peppermint (*Mentha × piperita*)	6-9	leaves	damp soils	peren	pl 4-5	tea
wild camomile	6-10	see **Stomach/digestion**				tea
Stomach/digestion						
milfoil, yarrow (*Achillea millefolium*)	6-9	shoot tips	dry meadows	peren	pl 5	tea
wild camomile (*Matricaria chamomilla*)	6-10	flowers	open farmland	ann	sd 4	tea
red bergamot (*Monarda didyma*)	6-10	leaves and flowers	garden bed	peren	ct 4	tea

Herbs for the home medicine cabinet (continued)

Stomach/digestion (continued)

caraway *(Carum carvi)*	7-8	seed	meadow, garden bed	bien	sd 5-8	tea, flavouring
garlic *(Allium sativum)*	8-9	cloves	average garden soil	peren	cloves 3-4 or 8	flavouring
fennel *(Foeniculum vulgare)*	8-10	seed	garden bed	peren	sd 4	tea
angelica *(Angelica archangelica)*	9-10	root	damp meadows and hedgerows	peren	sd 10, pl 4	tea, herb spirit

Blood cleansing

dandelion *(Taraxacum officinale)*	4-8	leaves	meadows	peren	gl 3-4, pl 5	tea
wild pansy, heartsease *(Viola tricolor)*	5-9	flowering plant with roots	fields and open soil	bien	sd 6-7	tea
great burdock *(Arctium lappa)*	10-11	roots	rubbish tips	bien	sd 6-7	tea

Nerves (calming)

lemon balm *(Melissa officinalis)*	5-10	shoot tips and leaves	garden bed	peren	ct 4-5	tea
lavender *(Lavandula angustifolia)*	6-7	shoot tips with flower buds	garden bed	peren	ct 4-5 or 10	tea, bath
St John's wort *(Hypericum perforatum)*	around 24.6	flowering plant	path edges, hedgerows	peren	sd 4	tea
fennel	8-10	see **Stomach/digestion**				tea
valerian *(Valeriana officinalis)*	9-10	roots	damp meadows and edges	peren	sd 4-5	tea

Wounds

comfrey *(Symphytum officinale)*	4-5 or 10-11 (5-10)	roots (leaves)	damp meadows	peren	pl 5	mash for poultices, ointment
ribwort plantain milfoil, yarrow	4-10 6-9	see **Respiratory tract** see **Stomach/digestion**				leaves for poultices
wild camomile great burdock	6-10 10-11	see **Stomach/digestion** see **Blood cleansing**				tea for compresses

Key: 1-12 = months of the year; sd = sowing direct; gl = sowing under glass; pl = planting;
ct = cuttings; ann = annual; bien = biennial; peren = perennial

Wild herbs that can protect other plants

Field horsetail
(Equisetum arvense)

Description: This perennial weed grows on open, moist, heavy soils. Up to April it produces only fertile, spore-bearing stems, and after that sterile stems like tiny fir trees.

Harvest: Remove above-ground shoots from May until August. They contain lots of silicic acid, which strengthens the resistance of other plants.

Tansy
(Tanacetum vulgare)

Description: Yellow inflorescences grow all summer, rising 40 in (1 m) above the fern-like leaves. Tansy grows well on dry path and woodland edges, and on banks; it spreads rapidly.

Harvest and properties: The above-ground shoots contain poisonous thujone among other things; harvest in July/August.

Male fern
(Dryopteris filix-mas)

Description: A perennial fern bearing funnel-shaped fronds, double-feathered and up to 40 in (1 m) long. Spores form on their undersides in summer.

The silicic acid contained in the field horsetail strengthens the resistance of other plants.

Position: Grows in the shade of deciduous woodland.

Harvest and application: The fronds contain substances that repel tapeworms and other parasites. But beware: male fern, even in small overdoses, can poison or blind. It can be harvested from June through until September.

Stinging nettle
See page 74.

Comfrey
See page 84.

Above *The shoots of the poisonous male fern form delightful 'bishop's crooks'.*

Tansy, despite its feathery, fern-like foliage, is in fact a close relative of the chrysanthemum.

Wild camomile
See page 80.

Garlic
See page 55.

Horseradish
See page 56.

Wormwood
See page 60.

93

Herbal preparations

Fermentation

Soak the herb in rainwater in a non-metallic container. After one to four weeks, the unpleasant smells subside. This means that fermentation has been completed.

Much diluted, the fermented liquid can now be sprayed over leaves.

Herbal preparations are one way of ensuring healthy and abundant growth.

Liquid fertilisers

Plant	Type	Quantity of fresh herb oz/pt (g/l)	Dilution	Nutrients
field horsetail	broth	2-4 oz (100-200 g)	1:10	silicic acid
stinging nettle	fermentation	2 oz (100 g)	1:(10-20)	nitrogen trace elements
comfrey	fermentation	2 oz (100 g)	1:20	nitrogen trace elements
wild camomile	cold-water extract	1 oz (50 g)	1:5	generally strengthening

Herbal preparations to combat pests and diseases

Plant	Type	Quantity of fresh herb oz/pt (g/l)	Dilution	Combats
field horsetail	broth	3 oz (150 g)	1:5	fungal diseases
stinging nettle	cold-water extract	2 oz (100 g)	neat	aphids
oak	fermentation of leaves	2 oz (100 g)	1:(5-10)	insect pests including ants
wild camomile	tea from flowers	¼-½ oz (10-20 g)	neat	used to disinfect seeds (strengthening)
garlic	tea	¼ oz (10 g)	1:10	fungal diseases
horseradish	broth from leaves	1 oz (50 g)	neat	brown rot on fruit
tansy	tea	½ oz (30 g)	1:(2-3)	sucking insects including mites
wormwood	fermentation	½ oz (30 g)	neat	sucking insects caterpillars, ants
male fern	broth or fermentation	2 oz (100 g)	1:10	sucking insects

Broth

Soak the plant materials in water for 24 hours, then bring everything up to the boil over a low heat, taking 20-30 minutes to do so. After the mixture has cooled, strain it and dilute as required.

Cold-water extract

Allow the plant material to stand for 24 hours in cold water. Then wring it out (to extract as much liquid as possible) and strain the liquid before it starts to ferment.

Tea

Pour boiling water over the chopped herb, cover it and allow to draw for about 15 minutes; then strain the liquid.

Index